Curtis C. Mitchell
Phil 1:6

let's live!

CHRIST IN EVERYDAY LIFE

CURTIS C. MITCHELL, Th.D.

let's live!

CHRIST IN EVERYDAY LIFE

FLEMING H. REVELL COMPANY
OLD TAPPAN, NEW JERSEY

All Scripture quotations in this volume are from the King James Version of the Bible.

Library of Congress Cataloging in Publication Data

Mitchell, Curtis C
  Let's live! Christ in everyday life.

    1. Christian life—1960–   I. Title.
BV4501.2.M54   248'.4   74–16153
ISBN 0–8007–0716–8

TO
My students at Biola College, both
past and present, whose constant questions
have greatly aided in developing the
concepts in my book

Contents

Introduction

The thesis of my book is that the philosophy of life set forth on the pages of the New Testament is *practical*. It is a life that can be lived by the average American in the average community today. One need not climb a mountain and contemplate his navel in order to live authentic New Testament Christianity.

I emphasize *what* Christian living really is and *how* it can be lived in plain practical terms. Each chapter deals with relevant problems faced by the ordinary Christian. Our desire is to scratch where Christians really itch. In these discussions every effort will be made to be simple, practical, and biblical.

let's live!

CHRIST IN EVERYDAY LIFE

1

Basic Philosophy of Christian Living

What really is authentic Christian living? There is a great deal of confusion in this area today. Some people have the idea that living the Christian life is following certain rigid standards: reading your Bible every day, praying every day, and so forth. Others recoil against this and say, "No, that's legalism. Today we are under grace, not law!" or, "God loves you and you don't have to perform for God," or, "There are no commandments under grace." I hope to demonstrate in this chapter that neither of these positions really represents New Testament living.

Before we can understand what Christian living really is, we must understand what Christianity is all about. If you ask the average person on the street, "What do you think a Christian is?" most of them would say, "Well, a Christian is sort of a social misfit —the kind of a guy who doesn't do a lot of things that the average person thinks are okay. He's an oddball! Like the fellow who wears red socks, has blemishes, and doesn't read *Playboy*." To most people, Christianity is a very negative philosophy. Like the fellow who says, "I don't smoke and I don't chew, and I don't go with the girls who do." It would appear that if you don't do enough things, you become a Christian by osmosis. Well, if that's what a Christian is, then my dog is the best Christian you will ever see! He doesn't do any of those things!

I think we would all agree on one thing—that if anybody could

13

tell us what a Christian is, it ought to be the Lord Jesus Christ. In John 10:27, 28 He tells us what the basic difference is between a Christian and a non-Christian. Christ said, "My sheep hear my voice, and I know them, and they follow me: And I give unto them eternal life; and they shall never perish." Christ *gives* unto them eternal life. Is that negative or positive? It's positive. A person who is a Christian is a person who has been *given* something by God that the other fellow doesn't have, and that is this positive quality or component called eternal life. The Christian has something that no one else in all the world has except another Christian and that is eternal life. So authentic Christianity is essentially a positive philosophy.

But what is eternal life? If we were to kick this question around, someone would probably say that eternal life is "living forever," or "endless existence." However, if you really think about it, everybody is going to exist forever in heaven or hell. There is more to eternal life than existing forever! For instance, someone might say, "What is a car?" and a fellow might answer, "Well, a car is four wheels." To be sure, for a car to function it must have wheels, but there is more to a car than wheels and there is more to eternal life than existing forever. Again, let's allow Christ to answer the question. In John 17:3 Christ says, "And this is life eternal, that they might know thee the only true God, and Jesus Christ, whom thou hast sent." What is eternal life? Eternal life is *knowing* God. Eternal life is *knowing* Jesus Christ. You might think you have nothing to worry about then if you have been in a good evangelical church and know all *about* Jesus Christ. You know that God is all powerful, that He is pure Spirit, and that Jesus Christ is 100 percent God and 100 percent man. However, it is one thing to know all about Jesus Christ and another thing to *know* Him!

I can remember, as a teen-ager, back in the Pleistocene Age, going on a weekend retreat with a group of young people. The first night there, the guys were all checking out the girls to see if there was a young lady that they might be interested in getting to know.

In my day, we had kind of an underground system by which we could find out all we needed to know about a girl. We could find out her name, her age, where she lived, how much she weighed, and everything else we might want to know. Yet, there was a great difference between knowing all *about* the young lady and being introduced to her and knowing her personally.

It is not, "Do you know all *about* Jesus Christ, but do you know Him personally?" Can you say with the Apostle Paul, "I know whom I have believed" (2 Timothy 1:12). Until and unless you can say that, you do not really know what authentic New Testament Christianity is all about. Because "this is life eternal, that they might *know* thee the only true God. . . ." God's way then is a glorious positive relationship—really knowing Jesus Christ and getting to know Him better and better.

Most of you know all of this. We've discovered the reality of Jesus Christ, but now I would like to pose a question to you Christians. Where do your friends get the misconception that Christianity is just a lot of *don'ts?* Did they get this concept from reading the Bible? No, because in the first place they don't read the Bible, and second, it doesn't teach that concept anyway. Did they get it from reading commentaries? Most of them don't know what a commentary is! For better or for worse, the conception that the average person has as to what a Christian is, is gained by looking at your life and looking at mine. We may be the only Bible he ever reads. Evidently, the things that stand out in our lives are the things that we *don't* do. Because of this, our unsaved friends come to the conclusion that Christianity is a lot of don'ts.

I am persuaded that just as the average unsaved person has a total misconception of what a Christian is, so the average Christian today is laboring under a delusion as to what Christian living really is and how you live it. If I were to ask you to state in a sentence or two your formula for living your Christian life this next week, I wonder what you would tell me? An average Christian would reply something like this, "Well, first of all, I'll try not to dip snuff, I'll try not to lie, I'll try not to tell dirty jokes, and so forth." He has a list of about twelve don'ts: the "dirty dozen." His idea of living a successful Christian life is to go through a week and not violate one of the dirty dozen. If he does this he's lived the Christian life. If he can go for two weeks without violating one of the dirty dozen, then he's really beginning to make progress. If he can go for a month without violating one of them, he is really getting to be a supersaturated saint!

With this concept of Christian living, it's easy to see how a person looking at such a life can come to the conclusion that Christianity is a lot of don'ts! The things that really stand out in such a life are the things that he doesn't do. Thus, the unsaved person concludes that Christianity is negative. To be consistent, however, we ought to go right on down the line and say not only do we not drink or smoke or chew, but we also don't read our Bibles, we don't witness, and we don't pray. We just don't do anything!

It wouldn't hurt to dust off that old Bible once in a while. It ought to help us understand the true nature of Christian living. The Bible pictures Christian living under several figures of speech or analogies. In 1 Corinthians 3:9-17, Christian living is spoken of as a building program. When you receive Jesus Christ as Saviour it's like having a foundation of a building laid in place of your life, and Christian living is erecting a superstructure on top of that foundation. In 1 Peter 2:2, 3 Christian living is pictured as a growing process. You start out as a little baby and you grow up. In 2 Timothy 4:7, the Christian life is like running the race. Let's analyze these statements.

How are buildings built—by doing things or by not doing things? How are races run? How do babies grow—by doing things or by not doing things? Let's say a mother has a baby and she wants it to grow healthy and strong. She says, "I am not going to feed my baby any arsenic, I'm not going to let it have any coffee. . . ." She lists twelve things she is not going to let her child experience. If that's all she does, how fast will the baby grow? It would shrivel up and die!

A man is going to erect a building and the contractor arrives one morning with fifty men. Before he allows these men to go ahead, he tells them that they are commissioned to build a building and says, "Men, here is how I propose to do it. I don't want any of you fellows to bend any nails. I don't want any of you sawing any boards crooked. I don't want any of you putting too much sand in the mortar." He goes on to list twelve things he doesn't want them to do. Those fifty men then set down and faithfully observe all of the don'ts. If that's all they did, how fast would the building go up?

By now you get the message! Buildings aren't built with don'ts. Babies don't grow on don'ts. Races aren't run with don'ts, and Christians can't live on don'ts. Ten thousand don'ts will never make you one bit more like the Lord Jesus. "Okay," you say, "isn't there a place for don'ts? Doesn't the Bible tell us not to do certain things?" Yes. It tells us not to lie, not to be proud, and so forth, but we need to understand the function of the negative. Referring back to the building, I'm sure you will agree that if it is going to be built, it has to be built essentially by the positive. Someone must drive nails and saw boards, and so forth. While I am building the building I will observe some negative rules. I'll try not to bend any nails and I'll try not to saw any boards crooked, but what is the function of the negative? I am observing these don'ts so as not to weaken the structure that I am building with the positive. But the sad thing is that many Christians think that they can build positive Christlike character by don'ts. They will never do it that way. You build with the positive and you observe negative rules so as not to weaken the positive character you are developing by the things that you do. *Christian living is essentially positive!*

If I were to close with this point you might say, "Now I've got the picture! I must get busy for Jesus. I'm going to start reading my Bible every day if it kills me (and it probably will), I'll pass out tracts every day, go to church every Sunday, join committees, sing in the choir, and generally get busy." Whenever some people feel their spiritual life slipping, they think the answer lies in increased religious activity. However, I can think of at least one woman in the Bible who was doing an awful lot for Jesus but was not becoming more Christlike in the process. Her name was Martha. She was very busy. The Bible says that she "was cumbered about much serving" (Luke 10:40), but was she becoming more Christ-like in the process? No, she became harsh and bitter. She came to Jesus with her bottom lip hanging out and said, "Lord, dost thou not care that my sister hath left me to serve alone?" (v. 40). Here is a case where doing things for Jesus did not make a person develop Christian character. I dare say that some of you have tried that route, and you've gotten so busy in church activity "for Christ" that you have become frustrated and yet you did not really develop in your Christian life.

Most Christians are living their Christian lives by a combination of do's and don'ts. We have certain things we do each day and certain things that we don't do. Our idea of living effectively is to follow rigidly a routine of do's and don'ts. We have the idea that if we are successful in observing all of our do's and abstaining from all of the don'ts, we are successfully living the Christian life.

I dare say some of you have been trying this route and you are *empty* inside! There is a basic fallacy in all of this. It's a fallacy that has been plaguing the church down through the years, and it's called *legalism.* You may be thinking that you have had good Bible teaching along this line and you may say you are no longer under law but under grace. Yet, I find that an awful lot of people who say that with their mouths are, in practice, living by law. They have fallen from grace. They really don't understand what grace is all about.

Isn't this really the same philosophy that the Pharisees were following? They had reduced their religious experience to a little system of external do's and don'ts that they rigidly tried to follow.

They would go to the synagogue at certain times, they would abstain from some kinds of meats, they would wash their hands a certain way, they would abstain from some people, and their idea was to become ever more proficient at their little routine of do's and don'ts.

Now, the only difference between the Pharisees and many Christians today is that our do's and don'ts are different. The same basic philosophy is there. To become ever more proficient at your do's and don'ts, and become like a trained seal going through your little routine each week, is not authentic New Testament Christianity, but *legalism*. If there is anything that the Bible is against, it's legalism. Read the Epistle to the Galatians.

The more I study the New Testament the more I discover that the Christian life is not a legal relationship but one of love. In John 3:16 we find that ". . . God so loved the world, that he gave his only begotten Son . . ."; Romans 5:8: "But God commendeth his love toward us, in that, while we were yet sinners, Christ died for us." Look at the outstanding characteristics of the really great men of the Bible. David, a man after God's own heart, says, "As the hart panteth after the water brooks, so panteth my soul after thee, O God" (Psalms 42:1). Here's a man in love with God. In Philippians 3:10, Paul says, "That I may know him, and the power of his resurrection, and the fellowship of his sufferings, being made conformable unto his death." In Philippians 1:21, Paul says, "For to me to live is Christ. . . ." You can't read words like that without realizing that here was a man who was really enthusiastically in love with Jesus Christ. The outstanding thing about the life of David and the life of Paul was not the do's and don'ts, but here were men who really had a heart for God. In 1 Corinthians 13 we are told that if we do not have love we are nothing. We can have all kinds of knowledge, we can speak with the tongues of men and angels, we can give our body to be burned, but if we don't have love we are a big zero. Christianity is not a legal relationship but a love relationship.

What is the difference between a legal relationship and a love relationship? Great confusion exists on this issue today. According to some, to live by grace (or love) is to be free from any and all commandments. We are told that one does not need to perform for God! God loves us regardless of how we act. I am afraid that these people forget that because God does love us, He is very much concerned with how we act. He loves us too much to allow us to continue to violate His commands. He is lovingly interested in our development. No, freely flaunting God's commandments is *not* living by love. Love is not license.

So then what is the difference between law and grace? The difference is *not* in what you do or you don't do, but in *motivation*—why you do what you do! A legal relationship is motivated by fear and reward. You do what you do because you're afraid you'll get fired, or you won't get your paycheck. Grace is motivated by love. For example: What is the difference between a housemaid and a housewife? I have never had a housemaid, but they tell me that you can hire one who will make the beds. Well, that's what my wonderful wife does. You can hire a housemaid who will wash the dishes, but my sweetheart does that, too. A housemaid will mop the floors, but my first lady humbles herself to that task as well. If you just looked at the do's and don'ts around the house, you could almost come to the conclusion that there is no difference between a housemaid and a housewife! But there is! Not in what they do, but in *why* they do what they do.

Not every woman who has a marriage license is functioning as a housewife. Some of them are legally married but they are functioning like a housemaid. The woman who is really functioning as a housewife will tell you there is a great deal of difference. The difference is *motivation*. The housemaid is operating under legal contract. If she doesn't do her job well, she'll get fired—fear and reward! But why does a housewife do those same things? It's because she loves her husband and her family. One is a legal relationship and the other is a love relationship. One is law, one is grace.

Let me ask you a basic question. Why did you read your Bible today? Why did you pray? Was it because you have been led to believe one way or another that to be a good Christian you have to read your Bible every day? A chapter a day to keep the devil away, so to speak? Or that some terrible plague will come upon you or that God will strike you with leprosy, the Hong Kong Colic, or the Korean Crud? If that's why you did it, you may say with your mouth, "I am living by grace," but you have fallen from grace. You are living by law!

Christianity is a love relationship between you and another person, Jesus Christ. The big problem is not the area of the do's and don'ts, but in maintaining that love relationship with consistency. If you are successful in maintaining a high love relationship with Jesus Christ, you don't need to worry about the do's and don'ts. They'll take care of themselves. It's impossible to separate love from deeds. In John 14:15, Jesus said, "If ye love me, keep my commandments." In John 14:23, He said, "If a man love me, he will keep my words." If you really love somebody, you desperately want to please them. Don't tell me that you love Jesus if you're flaunting His commandments! Don't just sit around strumming on a guitar, singing syrupy words about how you love Jesus, and continue to flaunt His commandments! You betray the very basic nature of love. You don't really know what love is all about. It is the nature of love to want to please the person you love. You show me a woman that really loves a man, and I'll show you a woman that desperately wants to please that man and vice versa.

If you really love Jesus Christ you don't need to worry about what you're going to do and what you're not going to do, because you are going to want to do the things that please Him. That's why Augustine said so many years ago, "Love God and do as you please." Why? Because if you really love God, you will desperately want to please Him. This is where it's at in the Christian life —maintaining this love relationship. If your love for Him is what it should be, everything else in your Christian life will fall into line.

I've spoken at many summer conferences and have observed

numerous camp romances. When a junior-high-school boy falls in love it is really something to behold. He walks around in a trance! He will do anything to please her, including walking off the pier if that's what she wants. That's the nature of love. If he detects anything in his behavior that is distasteful to that sweet young thing, he'll quit it.

It's impossible to love God and not want to please Him. It's impossible to love Him and not have the do's and don'ts. However, it is possible to have the do's and don'ts and not really love Him. That is legalism. The glorified Christ wrote a letter to a local church at Ephesus. He commended them for their zealous activity and their strict adherance to orthodoxy. They had the do's and don'ts in abundance. Yet, He went on to say, "Nevertheless, I have somewhat against thee, because thou hast left thy first love" (Revelation 2:4). The do's and don'ts were all proper and precise, but He said there was something wrong. They didn't love Him. He goes on to say that if the condition isn't straightened up He will snuff out their testimony! When love goes, the heart of the Christian relationship is ripped out, even if the do's and don'ts continue. Yet, the natural tendency in the Christian life is to reduce Christian living to a series of external do's and don'ts. Outwardly we may look like we are doing all of the right things, but we're empty inside.

Your basic task in your Christian life is to maintain a high-level love relationship between you and the Lord Jesus. If you are successful in this, everything else in your Christian life will fall into line. But when we speak of maintaining a love relationship, some people think of an effortless process. When the average teen-ager thinks of love he thinks of boy meets girl, birds singing, heart palpitation, moon in June. What could be more effortless than falling in love? Likewise, some Christian books in recent years have correctly presented Christian living as a love relationship, but in so doing, the picture is presented as an easygoing, hang loose, effortless sort of life. Such attitudes betray a very immature concept of love. Ask any successful married couple who have been married over a year and they will tell you that for two people to maintain a meaningful love relationship over the long haul, it's work. It is worth it, but it's work. And this is where the work comes into the Christian life. You have to work at the business of loving Jesus Christ. If you are going to stay in love with Him you are going to have to work at it.

What is the secret of maintaining a love relationship? What is the key? Almost all books on marriage come back to one basic concept as the key for two people maintaining a high-level love relationship with each other. That is *communication.* You show me a man and woman who are not communicating, and I'll show you a love relationship that is going to be in trouble. They may still stay married, but when love goes, the real heart of that relationship goes. You've got to communicate with a person to stay in love with him or her. Now the same thing is true between you and Jesus Christ. You are a person and He is a Person. If you are going to stay in love with Him, you are going to have to communicate with Him. I'm not saying you have to read your Bible every day, but you do have to communicate with Him daily, or something is going to happen to your love. I'm not saying you have to pray every day, but you have to communicate with Him every day.

This puts a different perspective on the do's and don'ts. It's not a question of saying legalistically, "Am I reading my Bible every day?" but, "Am I communicating by this process?" It is not a question of, "Am I praying every day?" but, "Am I communicating with my Lord?" I hope you went to church last Sunday, but let me ask you a question. Did you worship? Worshiping God is not just sitting inside a building and going through a routine. You can go in that building and sit there through the service and walk out an hour later and never have worshiped your God. Our public worship services should be looked upon as a *means* by which we communicate with God. But it takes effort to communicate. It is easier to just sit in church and let our minds go in neutral, but it takes concentration and discipline in order to really worship God.

The trouble is that we make prayer, Bible study, public worship, and so forth, ends in themselves instead of means to an end—means by which we communicate. As we communicate with Him, we fall more and more in love with Him. You cannot communicate consistently with Jesus Christ and not love Him. As you love Him the do's and don'ts will fall in line. You will want to please Him. You will want to abstain from the things that displease Him. It forms a glorious circle. As we communicate with Him we love Him, as we love Him we want to do things that please Him and abstain from the things that displease Him, and as we do these things it makes for more and better communication. It just keeps getting better and better. But let me remind you that communication takes work. The key then is *love.* And the key to love is *communication.* Think communication!

Psychologists tell us that there are certain things necessary for two people to communicate with each other. These we will call keys to communication. One key is *desire.* For two people to stay in love with each other they must want to. If they really don't have a strong desire they won't be willing to sacrifice and work at communication. The same thing is true in the Christian life. In Matthew 5:6 Christ said, "Blessed are they which do hunger and thirst after righteousness." Paul said, "I have not yet attained but I press on toward the mark . . ." (*see* Philippians 3:13, 14). Here is desire. If you no longer have this desire, frankly admit it to the Lord and ask Him to create it in your heart again.

The second key is *confidence.* The psychologists tell us that if two people are going to communicate with each other they have to have confidence in each other. Now confidence is simply a synonym for the good old biblical word *faith.* In Colossians 2:6 we are told, "As ye have therefore received Christ Jesus the Lord, so walk ye in him." How did you receive Jesus Christ? By faith. By putting your faith and confidence in what He has done to save you. We are to live our Christian life moment by moment by the same principle. In Galatians 2:20 we read, "I am crucified with Christ: nevertheless I live; yet not I, but Christ liveth in me: and the life which I now live in the flesh I live by the faith of the Son of God, who loved me, and gave himself for me." This is learning to rely moment by moment in Jesus Christ and His power within us. What does the Bible mean by living by faith? Living by faith does not mean a passive existence as some would imply. It does not mean "I do nothing."

The Christian life is not passive existence but active utilization of the power of God. This weekend I'm to speak at a conference in the mountains. How am I going to get to the mountains? I'm not going to run up there on my own strength. I will rely upon the power of the automobile; but when I say I rely upon the power of the automobile, that doesn't mean I relax in the back seat and say, "Automobile, take me up to the mountains." I have to steer, I have to turn on the ignition, I have to brake, but yet I'm not doing it in my own strength, I am utilizing actively the power of the automobile. Now that's living by faith. It's moment-by-moment dependence on Him, utilizing His power. Perhaps your communication is breaking down because you lack a vigorous confidence in the Lord. In a subsequent chapter we will fully discuss what biblical faith is and how it can grow.

The third key is *commitment.* Psychologists tell us that if two people are going to remain in love with each other they have to be dedicated to each other. They have to be committed to each other. The Bible teaches that dedication is absolutely necessary. "I beseech you therefore, brethren, by the mercies of God, that ye present your bodies a living sacrifice, holy, acceptable unto God, which is your reasonable service" (Romans 12:1). This, friend, speaks of commitment. Total commitment! There must be a complete total dedication of your life. Perhaps this is why you are not communicating with the Lord. You are holding out on Him. I make it a practice to remind myself daily of my commitment to Him; and if necessary, during the day. It is impossible to communicate deeply with someone to whom you are not wholly dedicated. Maybe that's why you're not communicating with God.

The fourth key is *honesty.* When one person begins to be dishonest with the other, then meaningful communication breaks down. What would be a biblical term for being honest with the Lord? "If we confess our sins, he is faithful and just to forgive us our sins, and to cleanse us from all unrighteousness" (1 John 1:9). That's nothing more than being honest with God. It's ridiculous not to be honest with God; He knows what's going on anyway. Yet, God wants a basic honesty from us if we are going to have meaningful communication.

Check out your desire. Do you really want to love God? Do you really have confidence in God? Are you really totally committed to Him? Have you been honest with Him? Any or all of these may be reasons why your communication has broken down and your Christian life is just a dull routine—a drag.

Would you like to be more like Jesus Christ 365 days from now, possessing more of the positive character of Jesus in your life? I'm sure you would answer *yes!* Perhaps you have tried many times before and feel that it is impossible. Let me give you a formula. It's not my formula, it's word for word from the Scripture. If you do this for the next 365 days, you have a money-back guarantee you will be more like Jesus Christ. It sums up in one concise statement all I have been trying to get across. It is found in 2 Corinthians 3:18: "But we all, with open face beholding as in a glass [literally *mirror,* and refers symbolically to the mirror of God's Word] the glory of the Lord." Now this is not just legalistically reading the Bible each day, but rather looking into the Word and beholding His glory! That's communication! That's real worship! Now if you do that consistently something is bound to happen. "You will be changed" (*see* v. 18). You cannot communicate with Jesus Christ every day for 365 days and be the same. You have to change. The tense of the verb here indicates a gradual change. You could translate it, "We are gradually being changed." As you consistently behold His glory and look into the mirror of God's Word and communicate with Him, you will gradually be changed. What is the nature of the change? We are, ". . . changed into the same image [the image of our wonderful Lord] from glory to glory even as by the Spirit of the Lord" (v. 18). As you really communicate with Him through His Word, through prayer, through worship service, through meditation, the Holy Spirit will gradually change you and make you like Jesus Christ. That's what Christian living is all about! Think communication!

2

The Hour That Can Change Your Life

In the previous chapter we demonstrated that biblical Christianity is essentially a love relationship between the believer and Jesus Christ. We saw that the key factor in maintaining any love relationship is communication. For two people to stay in love they must communicate. The very best way to guarantee daily communication with Christ is to set aside a time daily for private devotions. I am not saying that this is the only way to communicate with the Lord, but it is the most important way. I really don't believe anyone can grow and develop spiritually over the long haul without a consistent time of meaningful private devotions.

Now this personal time of devotional study is more than just having a Bible; it's more than just carrying a Bible around with you. Lugging a Bible around almost seems to be a status symbol with us. It's more than simply listening to Bible sermons or listening to Bible tapes. It's actually the spoken Word in our daily life. Daily communication is consciously shutting yourself off, consciously saying, "What does He want to tell me today?" Unless this is happening, and you are really communicating, I think everything else is rather shallow in your Christian life.

I know you've heard talks and lessons on personal devotions. You have been challenged to have devotions. You are probably familiar with the many verses of Scripture pointing up the importance of God's Word for spiritual growth and purity.

In my opinion, most evangelical Christians know full well the importance of a daily quiet time. In fact, most feel guilty for not consistently observing one. No, you probably don't need another fight talk on the subject. You want and need a practical, workable method for meaningful devotions.

In this chapter we want to put the emphasis on *how* to do it. So many times I think that we as Bible teachers and preachers are guilty of just challenge, challenge, challenge, but we never get around to telling people in a practical way how to do the things we challenge them to do. So I want to share with you a method that I have personally found very successful. I have shared it with my freshmen students at Biola College for a number of years. (The procedure set forth herein is very similar to that found in Stephen Olford's booklet *Manna in the Morning.* I had actually been teaching this method myself before this similarity was brought to my attention. Dr. Olford's booklet is very convenient to give to friends who need direction in this specific area.) I have had former students tell me time and time again what a benefit this simple procedure has been in their lives. They've told me that for the first time they are able to have meaningful devotions with consistency. Once a family man, with whom I had earlier shared this procedure, grabbed my hand warmly and, with great emotion, said, "I want you to know that that message did change my life and my relationships with my family."

So I really believe that this can be the hour that can change your life!

Equipment

To have a meaningful time of daily devotions necessitates certain equipment. First of all you must have a good Bible. By *good Bible* I mean one that is handy in size, not one of those monsters that some Bible salesman pushed off on the unsuspecting wife. You know, the kind that is so big that it almost breaks your coffee table with its weight! You need one that is not only handy in size, but *readable*—not print that is so small it takes a magnifying glass to read it. However, the main requirement for a Bible for devotional reading is *understandability,* one that you can really understand. If the King James English is hanging you up, don't fight it! Go down to your local Bible bookstore and tell them that you want to look at various translations. You will probably be shown a dozen translations or paraphrases. Just look through them and see which one speaks to you. Find one you can really understand and buy it!

For this type of Bible reading I do not recommend a Bible that has any marginal reference or footnotes. For example, I wouldn't recommend a Thompson's Chain Reference or Scofield Reference Bible for this type of reading. Please don't misunderstand me, I'm not downgrading reference Bibles at all. In fact, I've worn out about three or four reference Bibles, but for this type of Bible reading I just want the text of Scripture. I don't want any footnotes because when I have them I have a tendency to let my eyes drop down and see what the editors are saying at the bottom of the page or in the center column. For personal devotional reading I don't want that, I want to hear *HIS* voice, I want to listen to what God is telling *me* personally.

You should also have a good *loose-leaf notebook.* The one I use at present is probably six inches by eight inches, but it can vary in size somewhat. I'm going to discuss later how to maintain a personal spiritual diary. I have found it to be an extremely practical habit.

A third piece of equipment you will need will be a *prayer list.* We're going to devote a subsequent chapter to this subject. Several pages of your loose-leaf notebook can function as a prayer list. I have divided mine into the days of the week—a page for each day. At any rate, you will need to keep an up-to-date list of matters that really concern you.

Another matter which conceivably can be categorized as

equipment would be a proper *place* to observe your private devotions. The most important aspect of physical environment is to have a place away from noise as much as possible. A study of the life and teachings of the Saviour will validate this preference. For His times of private, serious communication with the Father, Christ preferred solitude. He would climb a mountain, or go out into the wilderness. It was not the ascetic value of such places that attracted Him at such times, but their *solitude.* In fact, Christ instructed His followers to seek the solitude of a closet for times of serious prayer.

Now for some of you, finding such a place will be easy, but for others it will be most difficult. Ask God to aid you in the matter. I am quite sure He will. It need not have significant ascetic qualities. I've known of people using such places as attics and garages. Again, the significant matter is solitude.

Time

Another matter that is extremely important but cannot rightly be listed as physical equipment is the matter of *time.* The program I have in mind will require at least one-half hour each day. If your relationship with Jesus Christ is not worth a half hour a day, then forget it. I really don't think that your Christian life is very significant to you if you are not willing to take a half hour a day to really make a serious effort to communicate with your Lord.

Now remember, it won't be easy! The devil will never allow it to be easy. I wish I could tell you, "Now I have been keeping a personal devotional time for twenty years and I can report to you that it has become almost an effortless process," but it hasn't. It is just as difficult today as it was when I began. I've made a practice of asking devout men if their devotional life became easier over the years—men whose lives were obviously being used of God. I would ask them, almost hoping they would assure me that it had, yet they always assured me it had not. Again, let me assure you that the devil will never allow it to be easy because he knows how important it is to you and to your spiritual development.

So, put it down that it is going to be difficult! You are going to have to *make* time. *Jesus made time!* Study His life: He missed breakfast if necessary; He would miss sleep if necessary. That should impress us, should it not? Jesus made time to get alone with God. If He felt that it was that important, if He needed to make time for private devotion, *how much more* will we need it? You must realize that it will take real determination. You are going to have to make up your mind that nothing short of the Rapture will keep you from your devotional time. When that predetermined time arrives, then no matter what happens, you are going to observe your devotions. That's the kind of determination it is going to take. I cannot overemphasize this point.

By way of example, some years ago I determined that I needed a certain time of physical activity each week. I decided to set a certain number of hours aside each week to play handball. Whenever that time comes I just drop everything. I don't care how full my desk may be, I just drop it and go. Some of my colleagues have tried to start such a program, but they have always fallen by the wayside because of a lack of determination. The time would arrive, but they wouldn't go because they had a lot of work to do. You must make up your mind and set some priorities. Regardless of how busy you may think you are, you must *take* the time. That's the kind of determination it is going to take.

There will be times when you won't feel like it. There will be times you won't want to do it. There are times when I have my private devotions that I just feel plain mean! At such times, I just tell the Lord how I feel and proceed. We must be honest with Him. It is really stupid not to be honest with Him because He knows what is happening anyway. My point is that when the predetermined time arrives, *nothing* must be allowed to interfere.

So far as the particular time of the day is concerned, I think that morning is best. Some people recommend the evening, but I want to talk to my Commander-in-Chief before the battle begins, not after the battle is over. To observe your private devotions at the end of the day is like having your car tuned up after you've taken the trip. So I prefer the morning, before the activities of the day. However, if you are a night person and you function differently, set up a time and determine that you are going to keep it.

It always amuses me when people say that they don't have time for private devotions. They usually have time to watch television and read the sports section. We have time for the things that we really think are important. Actually you will find that a consistent observance of private devotions will be a great *time-saver.* Does not God tell us that His Word is a "lamp unto our feet, and a light unto our path?" (*see* Psalms 119:105). Have you ever been in the mountains at night without a light? At such a time a flashlight is a tremendous time-saver! Without a light a person stumbles around all over the place. All of this reminds me of a fellow who pulled up in front of his friend's house. The house was all dark inside and he almost didn't go to the door, but he proceeded to ring the doorbell anyway. A voice from within says, "Yes?" The friend replies, "Is that you, Charlie?" Charlie's friend replies, "Yes, come on in!" The man enters the darkened room and asks, "What are you doing?" The man in the darkened room responds, "I'm looking for my fountain pen." Charlie replies, "Why don't you turn on the light?" His friend replies, "I can't, I haven't got time, I'm too busy looking for my fountain pen." I'm sure you can see the obvious point of the story. I challenge you to begin to turn on the light every day and it is going to save you time in the long run.

Attitude

Attitude is very crucial in successful devotions. You must approach it with an attitude of *anticipation.* You can have the correct time, place, equipment, and all the rest; but if you do not approach it with real anticipation, the whole procedure will become just a little legalistic routine. There *must* be this attitude of anticipation and expectation. You must come eagerly expecting to communicate with God.

To have an attitude of real anticipation you must be *physically alert.* Let me be very practical. This means that if you are going to be physically alert at 6:30 A.M. each day, it will be impossible to watch a late TV show night after night that keeps you up till one or two in the morning and still communicate with God at 6:30 with the physical alertness necessary for an attitude of anticipation. Physically there is just no way you are going to do that, so it will mean that you are going to have to discipline your time. After all, just how important is this to you? If it's important enough, you'll be willing to turn off television a little bit earlier, or you'll be willing to come in from your activities a little bit earlier. It's really a matter of priorities. When a person is in training for football, the coach often places him under a curfew. Generally, young men think that it is really neat. They say to their date, "Sorry, baby, got to cut it off early tonight. I'm in training!" How important is your relationship to Christ? If it's really important, you're going to have to organize your time so as to be physically alert at the proper time in the morning. That may mean you will need to discipline yourself regarding studies and other activities. It will mean that some of you will need to make wiser use of your time during the day. We invariably make time for those activities we really deem important!

An attitude of alertness is also definitely related to the *position of the body.* I find it very difficult to be really alert while my body is in a horizontal position. I'm quite sure that you've had this experience as I have. The alarm rings at 6:30 and I begin to rationalize by saying, "Well, I'm sure I can communicate with God horizontally as well as vertically." So I scrunch the pillow up under my head, reach over to get my Bible, and start having my devotions horizontally. I've discovered that such a procedure is the surest possible cure for insomnia. It puts me to sleep faster than anything in the world. I don't know about you, but in order for me to be physically ready to communicate with God I must get out of that bed. I have to shave, brush my teeth, and eat breakfast before I am ready physically to meet with God with real anticipation. Now whatever you have to do to prepare yourself physically, do it.

Not only must we be ready physically, but we must be ready *morally* as well. We are going to be communicating with a *holy God!* Therefore, we must be morally clean to communicate meaningfully. David said, "If I regard iniquity in my heart, the Lord will not hear me" (Psalms 66:18). Christ taught us that if we are about to engage in worshiping God and become aware of something amiss between ourselves and another brother, we should first go and patch up things with our brother and then proceed with the worship experience (*see* Matthew 5:23, 24).

Actually, one of the keys to having effective communication between two people is *honesty.* For two people to communicate with each other they must be honest. If one or the other begins to be dishonest, meaningful communication begins to break down. So make sure that you are clean before God before beginning your private devotions. If you aren't, then apply 1 John 1:9 and confess the thing to the Lord. This is nothing more than being honest with God.

Proper Procedure

Having discussed the equipment and the attitudes, let us now turn our attention to the matter of procedure. You come expectantly to the proper place at the proper time with your Bible and notebook in hand—what do you do? How do you proceed? The following procedure is one I have used for years. I have passed it on to hundreds of people. Many have later told me that it is the only procedure they have ever used with success. It is by no means the only method. I share it with you hoping it will meet your need. Feel free to use as much as is helpful to you. Feel free to alter and adjust to your personality.

The first step is to *stop*. The first thing to do upon arrival at the place where you plan to have your devotions is simply to sit there for a few minutes and do absolutely nothing. That's why I call it stop. I read or heard somewhere once that hurry was the death of devotions. Five minutes unhurried before God is better than one hour when you are watching the clock. We live in such a busy world that unconsciously our metabolism is in high gear. I find that if I just go into my office, turn on the light, sit down with my desk full of things to do, and start immediately to have my devotions, my mind is saying, "Let's hurry up and get this over with so you can get at what is really important!" I find it's far better to sit there a while and do nothing. Just sort of relax in His presence. Allow yourself to calm down. Sit there quietly with your eyes closed for several minutes.

Some mornings you may find it very difficult to unwind. At such times I've found it helpful to sing softly some old familiar hymn. In those moments I try to remind myself that Jesus is in that very room (*see* Matthew 28:20), and is willing to communicate with me. Often I tell myself that this is the most important thing I will be doing all day long! What could possibly be more important than a personal, private interview with the Lord Jesus Christ?

Speak. Now we are ready to pray. Prayer must be a vital part of any meaningful time of consistent daily devotions. Because we have an entire chapter devoted to this subject, I will not use a great deal of space to discuss it now. I will simply say that when it comes time to pray, pour out your soul to God in an uninhibited manner. Tell Him if you feel terrible. Praise Him for the things He has done. Relate to Him the things that are on your heart that you desperately need. Get out your prayer list and go over the matters that you are concerned about.

I find that it really helps my concentration to make my prayers audible. In fact, I like to walk up and down my office with my prayer list in hand and audibly lay before God the things on my list. This also assists in my need for daily exercise—sort of spiritual jogging. At times I find it helpful to imagine the Lord visibly present in the room assuring me that He will consider any and all matters and deal with them in the best possible manner.

The crucial issue in prayer is *heart concern.* If that is present, your prayers are getting through; but if that is lacking, you are wasting your time. Your mouth may be emitting sweet phrases—even pious phrases, but they are of no value.

Again, don't try to rush the procedure. Your best seasons of prayer will be when you become oblivious to the clock. Yet, on the other hand, don't try to artificially elongate your time of prayer. Pray as long as you have something of concern to say to your Lord and no longer.

I find it a helpful preparation toward the next step to close my time of prayer with a frank acknowledgment of my inability to comprehend spiritual truth, and a request for the Holy Spirit to teach me during my subsequent time of Bible meditation.

Look. With my heart and mind prepared by prayer, I am ready to look into the Word. For this type of reading, I read for quality, not for quantity. Don't try to set a goal of reading through the Bible in a year or anything of that nature. Don't even tell yourself you are going to have to read a chapter a day. Very seldom do I ever actually read a chapter during these sessions. In these moments I'm not trying to read through the Bible in a year, rather I am trying to see what *He is telling me!* I generally read a unit of thought. Sometimes I just read one verse, but usually it involves four or five. The Bible I use for my private devotions is a translation divided into paragraphs. I normally read a paragraph each morning. I go paragraph by paragraph through a book.

I read that paragraph three different times. Each time I read it slowly with my pencil in hand, underlining things that come to my attention. I read the first time to get the *general flow* of thought

—generally, what is said in that paragraph? Next, I read the second time to see *specifically* what is being taught in the paragraph. Finally, I read it a third time to see personally what the Lord is telling me. I find that by the time I get around to the third time, I am ready to hear His voice, so this time I read to see *precisely what He is trying to tell me!*

Recently I've experimented with using two versions of the Bible: reading the first time with Version *A;* the second time with Version *B;* and the third time with Version *A* again. I find it gives a stimulating breadth of illumination.

I have had students who have shared with me that they take a hymnal with them and supplement the Bible reading by reading the words of one of the great hymns. There is some meaty material in most old hymns. I've known of people who supplement Bible reading with a devotional book. However, I personally like to confine my reading to the Bible exclusively in my private devotions. In our house we do use devotional guides for family devotions in the evening, but for my private devotions I want to hear His voice. I think it is exciting to let Him tell me things directly from the Scripture. At any rate, there are all kinds of possibilities. Don't be afraid to experiment.

Think. The next step is to *listen.* By that we mean meditation. Think over what you have read, particularly those words or portions you have underlined. Biblical meditation is different from oriental mystical meditation. It is not throwing your mind into neutral. Rather it is rolling the Word of God over and over in your mind (*see* Psalms 1:2). The Hebrew word conveys the picture of a cow chewing her cud. As you roll these thoughts around, try, with the Spirit's help, to apply them in practical ways to your life. So often we apply God's Word to others. Try at this time to apply it to yourself. As you are meditating you might find it helpful to ask yourself certain questions such as: "Is there a command I've seen this morning that He wants me to obey? Is there a promise that He wants me to claim? Is there a sin that He is warning me to avoid? Is there a new truth that He wants me to learn?"

Again, do not rush this step. It can well be the most vital. As you roll these concepts around in your mind in an unhurried manner, you will begin to see various ramifications of the original thoughts. You will think of concrete ways to avoid the sins of which you have been warned. God will show you actual intermediate steps to achieve the ultimate goals stated in the passage. You will think of broader implications of the promises you have seen. Often we go through the mechanics of daily devotions, but lose much of the benefit because we don't take time to meditate! Develop this art. Allow yourself time to realize fully what He is trying to tell you. Ask Him to help you to remember them. There have been times when I have received an especially choice nugget and have written it on a three-inch by five-inch card and placed it in my shirt pocket. Then during the day I just pull it out and remind myself of the choice things He told me that morning. This is the way we learn, line upon line, precept upon precept, here a little, there a little. God gradually teaches us. It's vital.

Record. The next step is to write down your thoughts. This is a very important and very helpful step. This is where you take that loose-leaf notebook and keep a personal spiritual diary. At that moment write down in a personal way the things that God has told you—the burdens on your heart, the besetting sins that are bothering you, the prayers that He has answered, the truths He has revealed to you. Don't try to be flowery. Don't write it to impress others. Keep it intensely personal.

Even the mechanics of writing these things down helps to fix them in your mind. This personal, spiritual diary over the years can become a source of devotional material. When you are called upon to give a devotional, it is exciting to go back in your personal spiritual diary and see that God gave you something which you can share with others. I am not opposed to consulting commentaries, but the commentators do not have a corner on the truth. God can show you things, too. Write them down and as the occasion arises, share them with others.

Also, it will help you appreciate your spiritual progress. The great problem in the matter of consistent private devotions is that the benefits are *certain* but very *gradual.* It is much the same with the matter of eating nutritional food. We know that good eating habits will make for growth and health, but the benefits are realized very gradually. For example, a fellow may hear a lecture on nutrition, get all excited, go down to the health food store, buy a bunch of this health food and eat it faithfully three times a day for seven days. At the end of seven days he will notice no evidence of better health and say, "I've still got the same aches and the same potbelly. It's not doing any good." That is not a fair judge of the program. You must eat nutritious food longer than seven days to really evaluate whether it is doing you any good or not! If you try the program for a year, you will notice improvement, but not in seven days.

Perhaps a better illustration would be that of a small boy measuring himself against the wall to see how tall he is. Then the boy faithfully eats three good meals a day for seven days. At the end of the seventh day he again, in his childish logic, concludes that eating three good meals per day doesn't do him any good. Such logic is obviously fallacious! Mature people know that if the boy would undertake such a program for 365 days, he would notice a difference. After a year he would clearly realize that he has grown and made progress.

The same thing is true spiritually. Some of you are apt to try this program for a week with real enthusiasm and then childishly conclude that you haven't seen any development and so cast it aside. Don't evaluate the success or failure of this program by the experience of one week or one month.

I want to challenge you to try it for 365 days. Do exactly what I am telling you for 365 days and keep your personal spiritual diary. Don't look at it. Don't read it for 365 days, and at the end of a year read it. I promise you that you will be thrilled. I have had Biola students who have felt that their first year in college was a spiritual flop. Yet, they faithfully kept their spiritual diary. At the end of their freshman year they would go back and read it. Without fail they were surprised and thrilled. They say, "Lord, look what You have done, look what You have taken me through. I don't have this problem anymore—You've licked it." Then they would begin to appreciate the fact that they were making spiritual progress. Unless such a daily record is kept, you will never realize the progress you are making and therefore not be encouraged by it.

Share. A very important step is to share what God gives you. I want you to have one or two Christian brothers or sisters that you are going to share with regularly each day. What God gives you in the morning, share that very day. Ask God to give you someone in your shop or school to share with. Confine the sharing group to no more than four. Perhaps during the coffee break you can get together and share. I want to tell you that this is real "body life." This is encouraging one another. This is admonishing one another. This is exhorting one another to love and good works. This is real authentic New Testament Christianity. If one brother is absent, go out and find that brother. Keep each other going on this thing.

I want to tell you that daily sharing is a tremendous aid to consistency. My wife and I share each day. She is also my secretary and I go over to the school before my first class and have my devotions. She has her devotions at home. Then she starts working at 10:00 A.M. At 9:30 after my first class, we meet for coffee and share. You want to know a secret? There has been more than one morning when that alarm has gone off and I've said, "I'm tired this morning. I'm sure the Lord will understand if I don't have my devotions." About then a little light goes on in my brain and I say, "Now wait a minute, Mitchell, your wife is going to be meeting with you at 9:30 and she is going to expect you to have something to share." That simple fact has helped to keep me consistent in the program. It's the same principle that's found in Fat Girls Anonymous, or Weight Watchers, or Alcoholics Anonymous.

They get together and encourage each other regularly.

Follow. The final step is to conscientiously follow what the Lord reveals. All of these things that have been discussed lead to one word. *Obey.* I speak at various camps and conferences, and I hear a lot of speakers on the subject of Christian living. They all have their own little formula as to how to live the Christian life. While speaking at one of these Bible conferences, a lady who operated a bookstore said, "You know, I get a little mixed-up. You Bible teachers come up here each week and each time I hear a different formula on how to live the Christian life, I find myself getting confused." And you know something? She is right! Some of us call it one thing and some another. Some will speak of the "displaced life" or the "misplaced life." Others advocate taking "ten steps" or "five hops." Yet, if you analyze all of them they generally all get back to the words of the old hymn, "Trust and obey, for there's no other way to be happy in Jesus but to trust and obey." That's what it's really all about. If the Lord shows you truths, and He will, be careful to obey. He will not take you any deeper than you are willing to obey. I'm sure you've heard it stated: "Revelation and obedience are like the two parallel ties that make up a railroad track. When one stops the other stops."

Don't begin this program unless you want to assume responsibility! Yet, isn't that what maturity is really all about? As you mature in society you are expected to assume more and more responsibility. As you become mature spiritually, you are expected to assume more and more responsibility. So maturity and responsibility go hand in hand.

I honestly believe that this can be the hour that can change your life. I really believe that this can be the most important thing you can do each day. Now I grant you that if you're not careful it can become just another legalistic "do." As you are going through the process you must constantly remember that this program is simply a *means* by which you are going to communicate with your God. So *think communication!* You can go through this whole process and walk out a half hour later and never have communicated! These are not *ends* in themselves. They are *means* by which you communicate. I am persuaded that if you do this consistently for a year, it will make a difference. You cannot interact with God in this manner with consistency for one year and remain stagnant in your spiritual development. Gradually the indwelling Holy Spirit will change you. Ever so slowly He will develop the fruits of the Spirit in your personality (*see* 2 Corinthians 3:18).

3

The Tactics of Temptation

Temptation is a very real problem in the life of every Christian. In fact, I honestly believe that it is more of a problem to a Christian than a non-Christian. Before you were saved you were like a dead fish floating downstream with very little resistance. You were dead in trespasses and sin. You weren't trying to fight the devil, you were going along with his program. But if you can imagine that dead fish suddenly becoming alive and trying to swim upstream with a great deal more resistance, that's essentially what happens when we become Christian. And so temptation is a very real thing because we are bucking the tide of the devil's program. Ephesians 6:12 says, "... we wrestle not against flesh and blood, but against principalities, against powers. . . ." We are up against a highly organized enemy that has strategy, tactics, and battle plans. The trouble is that the average Christian approaches this whole procedure like a gang fight.

Now there is a difference between a gang fight and organized warfare. In a gang fight there are no plans, no tactics, and no strategy. You just start whaling away. In an organized battle, there are maneuvers, tactics, strategy, and overall plans. The problem as I see it is that the average Christian is going up against a highly *organized* enemy in a completely *disorganized* manner. We just blindly start fighting and then we wonder why we are consistently clobbered! It's because we don't study our battle manual (the

Bible) to familiarize ourselves with its battle strategies. Do you realize that there are times when fighting a temptation can be the very worst thing to do? Sometimes it is better to run from a temptation. There are different kinds of temptations, and different ways to handle them. God outlines these things in the Bible.

Now in a battle there are two factors that need to be considered. These are *power* and *strategy*. Both are crucial. If you don't have power you can't have victory in a battle, but you must also have proper tactical maneuvers. In this chapter the emphasis is on tactics rather than power. I find that most Christians are well instructed on the power aspect. It is simply utilizing the power of the indwelling Holy Spirit. However, even with adequate power, victory is not necessarily assured. You must use that power in the right way at the right time. That's tactics—that's strategy.

For example: Let's imagine an admiral on a battleship with all kinds of power at his disposal. He's attacked by an airplane and gives an order from the bridge: "Okay, men, throw over the *depth charges.*" He would be devastatingly defeated! Why? Because depth charges don't do anything against airplanes. They are designed to destroy submarines. Now in that case his defeat would not be due to a lack of power, but a failure in strategy.

This may sound ridiculous, but some Christians do things just as stupid nearly every day and then wonder why they get clobbered. When the Bible says run, they try to fight. When it says fight, they try to run, and then wonder why they are consistently defeated! There are different kinds of temptation and there are different ways that God says to handle these temptations.

Now when entering a battle, a good general wants to know two basic things. He wants to know what the enemy is going to throw at him, and he wants to know where he is vulnerable. So let's take up first of all the *source of temptation.* What is the enemy going to throw at us?

I think we can say that the ultimate source of all evil is Satan, the devil. But when we say that, that doesn't mean that the devil always attacks us personally. It would be kind of like saying that Hitler was behind all German aggression in World War II. Now when you make a statement like that it's true, but it doesn't mean that Hitler always attacked each GI personally. But when the German submarines sank our ships in the Atlantic, that was Hitler. When the German Panzer divisions rolled over France and Belgium, that was Hitler coming at us in various ways. By the same token, the devil comes at us through three basic channels. In Scripture these are called: the *world,* the *flesh,* and the *devil.*

So let's understand our enemy. Probably the easiest of the three to understand would be the *devil.* Scripture teaches that there is one personal supernatural spirit being known as the devil or Satan, probably the most powerful being that God ever created. He was originally created a high angelic being—most people think an archangel. He was given high responsibilities right at the headquarters of God. To make a long story short, he committed mutiny. He tried to overthrow God's government and take over. God booted him out of heaven. In his attempted coup, roughly a third of the angelic hosts of heaven were involved and thrown out with him. These are now called fallen angels, the devil's angels, or demons. So, when we say the word "devil" in this chapter, we mean either the one personal supernatural spirit being known as the devil, or, more probably, one of the millions of demons or fallen angels that do his bidding. Sometimes you are directly attacked by demons. I don't need to labor this point so much anymore with most people. It's amazing how the attitudes have changed towards demons and the spirit world in the seven years I've been teaching at Biola College. Seven years ago when I first started teaching and came across the first incident in the New Testament where Christ cast out a demon, the students looked at me as though I were something from the Middle Ages. They would say to me, "You don't really believe in demons, do you?" I had to go carefully into my Bible and show them that it really taught that there were such things as demons. Today, however, I don't even have to labor the point. I find that the present generation is acutely aware of the reality of the spirit world— much more so than my generation. Even on some secular campuses a person can get a degree by majoring in occult studies. In Oakland, California, they are offering a course in the occult to high-school students!

Now the second channel through which the enemy can attack is the *world*. The word *world* is used in various ways in the Bible. For example, in John 3:16 we read, "For God so loved the world. . . ." The word *world* is a reference to mankind. That's not the kind of world we are talking about. Sometimes the world means the planet Earth. That's not what we are talking about, either. The kind of *world* we are talking about in this chapter is the one mentioned in such Scriptures as 1 John 2:15, "Love not the world, neither the things that are in the world. If any man love the world, the love of the Father is not in him." Or, Romans 12:2, "Be not conformed to this world. . . ." Or, *see* James 4:4, "If any man is a friend of the *world* he is the enemy of God." Here is a world that is hostile. Here is a world that's our enemy. What kind of world is this that the Bible keeps warning us about? Let me give you a definition.

When the Bible uses the word *world* in this hostile sense, it means: *the world of unsaved men and the society, culture, and value systems that they have established.* In most American cities probably 80 percent of the people are unsaved. Who is ultimately controlling every unsaved man? Satan is! If you don't believe that, read Ephesians 2:1-3. Every unsaved man is walking "according to the course of this world, according to the prince of the power of the air. . . ." It really bothers me when I hear an unsaved person tell me that he is free. He is not free! Poor saps like him are like puppets on a string. When the devil says jump, they say, "How far?" without realizing it.

Now if 80 percent of the people in a community are demon controlled, who is establishing the culture in that town? Who is establishing the priorities? Who is setting the pace? *Demon dominated men!* That's why the Bible says that we are not to be conformed to this world. We are not to live by the same goals and purposes or have the same priorities and values. The most subtle kinds of temptation we deal with are from this channel—*the world!* Most of the time when you are tempted by the world, you are not tempted to do anything illegal or nasty; yet, it is devastating to your spiritual welfare.

For example: the last Sunday-school class I had before coming to teach at Biola College was a young-married-couples' class. I saw this incident happen several times. A young couple would be very zealous for the Lord and then all of a sudden I would begin to miss them in class. I would go out to check on what had happened and find that they had purchased a new home. Now is there anything immoral about buying a new home? Is there anything illegal about buying a new home? No! Well, in purchasing this house they would contract to buy it without the landscaping in order to save money. I think you can guess what happened. They became so involved in landscaping the house that they had no time for God and were actually loving that house more than they were loving God, and that is *sin.* That is idolatry!

Here was a perfectly moral, perfectly legitimate thing of the world that was devastating to their spiritual well-being. The Bible would put it this way, ". . . the love of money is the root of all evil" (1 Timothy 6:10). Brother, are we ever hassled by the world in our materialistic society today. The most difficult type of temptation you'll come up against comes from this source.

The final channel of temptation is the *flesh.* The word *flesh* is used a number of ways in the Bible. Sometimes it means the material body. Sometimes it means humanity. But the kind of flesh that we are talking about is the kind referred to in Galations 5:17, "For the flesh lusteth against the Spirit, and the Spirit against the flesh: and these are contrary the one to the other: so that ye cannot do the thing that ye would." Here is something that's my enemy. The *flesh* is also sometimes referred to as the "old man" in Romans 6. In Romans 7 it is referred to as the "sin that is in me." In Romans 8 it is called the "carnal man." What does it mean? It is referring to your old sin nature, that inborn selfishness and rebellion. You've got an enemy right on the inside. A traitor within the ranks of your own personality through which Satan can operate.

Where did we get this thing? We got it from our parents! And they got it from their parents, and so forth, right back to fallen, rebellious Adam who begat sons and daughters after his likeness and after his image (*see* Genesis 5:3, 4). The Bible teaches that parents pass on to their offspring not only *physical* characteristics: blond hair, blue eyes, and big feet, but also *spiritual* characteristics. That's why parents never have to teach their children how to be selfish! It just comes naturally.

Brother, do we ever have a battle on our hands! We must face this evil triad every day. Someone once said, "We have the *world* that's external, the *flesh* that's *internal,* and the *devil* that's *infernal,"* to deal with every day of our lives!

But, not only does a good general want to know what the enemy is going to throw at him, he also wants to know *where he is vulnerable.* He wants to know where he is subject to attack. Where am I vulnerable to attack by the enemy: the world, the flesh, and the devil? This is really asking the age-old philosophical question, "What are little girls made of and what are little boys made of?" The Bible really tells us. In 1 Thessalonians 5:23 we read, "And the very God of peace sanctify you wholly; and I pray God your whole spirit and soul and body be preserved blameless unto the coming of our Lord Jesus Christ." The whole man involves the *spirit, soul* and *body.* Any temptation you have will either be in the area of your spirit or in the area of your soul, or in the area of your body. You'll never be tempted any place else. Why not? Because that's all there is of you! So that simplifies matters.

Now let's understand ourselves. Of these three—spirit, soul, and body—the easiest to comprehend is the body. The body means the material you: the meat, the bones, the eyeballs. Some temptations are directed right at the biological drives of the body, and you are vulnerable in that area. Now in our culture, *sex* is probably the biggest temptation directed at the appetites of the body. We are living in a sex-saturated society. A Christian is constantly tempted to misuse and misdirect these biological drives that God has given us.

But that's not the only temptation that is directed to the appetites of the body. For instance, you get to my age and you're bothered with the battle of the bulge. Overeating is the same basic type of temptation. It's directed right at the biological drives of the body. And, contrary to public opinion, I personally feel that much of dope addiction and alcoholism is directed right at the biological drives of the body.

Now I realize that not everybody can have God's best. Not everyone can attend a Christian college. Some had to complete their education at a second-rate secular institution, and in those institutions students are usually told that the body is all there is to a man. Man is simply a machine. A biological machine. Man is the sum of his parts. Well, God says that actually the body is simply the house in which the essential person lives and operates, and the real you is nonmaterial. In fact 2 Corinthians 5 speaks of having a house that's decaying—a tent—and he (Paul) wants to move out of that tent to something better, referring, of course, to the physical body.

The *real you* is referred to in this chapter as spirit-soul. Most of the time these terms are used synonymously in Scripture. Together they make up the real you that's living in your body. And while most of the time they are synonymous, obviously in 1 Thessalonians 5:23 there is a distinction in some way between spirit and soul. Now in this specialized sense *only* what do we mean by *spirit* and what do we mean by *soul?*

First of all let's take the soul. Again, keep in mind that we are only using this word in a specialized sense, because sometimes soul means the whole person. But when the word *soul* is used in this specialized sense in contrast to the spirit, let me give you a definition. It means, essentially, the *self-consciousness.* That capacity that you have to say, "I." That capacity that you have that makes you aware of yourself in relationship to your environment. Animals are said to have souls. They have a certain degree of self-consciousness. Now how much I don't know; I've never had a personal talk with my dog, and I'm not even on speaking terms with my cat. Many temptations are directed right at your self-consciousness, because involved in that self-consciousness is this thing called pride or ego! And if you analyze your temptations, a great majority of them are directed at your ego.

What then do we mean by *spirit* in this specialized sense? Man was made by God to be aware of himself in his environment, but what else was man made to be aware of? Man was created to not only be aware of himself, but also to be aware of *God!* So let's call the spirit the "God-consciousness." Now this is something that is uniquely Homo sapiens. Animals have a certain degree of self-consciousness, but Scripture never ascribes any God-consciousness to animals. Man alone has a capacity for God. And wherever you find man, unless it has been deliberately educated out of him, you will find him trying to worship something. However, I don't believe that it can really be educated out of him. Why is it that you never find a cow trying to worship anything? It's because cows do not have this capacity.

Now, all temptation, when it's yielded to, becomes sin, and all sin affects your relationship with God. Not all temptation is directed right at your relationship with God, but some is. When you are tempted to deny God's goodness, when you are tempted to deny God's Word, when you are tempted to deny God's faithfulness, these are attacks right at your God-consciousness (spirit). A very common illustration of this type of temptation is usually experienced by new converts. A new Christian is especially vulnerable to attacks in his God-consciousness. After conversion he initially revels in his newfound salvation. Then someone on the job agitates him, and in a weak moment he whirls around and lets the other person have it! Perhaps some of his old vocabulary comes out! Right then the enemy attacks him. He says, "Look what you just said to that man. Is that the way a Christian ought to act? Let's face it, you're not really saved." Do you see what that is? That's an attack right at his God-consciousness trying to get him to doubt his relationship with God.

Now pay attention to this next statement. As you study your Bible you'll find that the *world* generally attacks you in the area of your *soul.* Why do you want money and the things that money will buy? Why do you want a better car, a better house to live in? If you really analyze it, you'll find that all too often you want these things so people will notice you: *ego!* So the world attacks you in the area of the self-consciousness. A direct demonic attack will be in the area of the spirit—the God-consciousness, doubting God's Word, doubting God's faithfulness, and so forth. When you are attacked in the area of the *body,* it will usually be coming from the old sin nature.

A. Devil $\longrightarrow$ Spirit
B. World $\longrightarrow$ Soul
C. Flesh $\longrightarrow$ Body

These are the three basic types of temptation. I call tham the *ABC*s of temptation: Type *A,* Type *B,* and Type *C.* Type *A,* the devil, attacks the God-consciousness or the spirit. Type *B,* the world, attacks your self-consciousness or the soul. Type *C,* the old sin nature, attacks the appetites of the body. Now I admit that the subject of temptation can be more complicated than this. Sometimes you could conceivably be attacked by two at once, but I've personally found it of great benefit if I get the *ABC*s down.

It is crucial when you are being tempted to determine what kind of temptation it is. Is it Type *A,* Type *B,* or Type *C?* There is a different way that each should be handled; and if you don't know what it is, you are not going to know how to intelligently deal with it. So, you must form the habit of determining what kind of temptation it is. Ask yourself, "What area of my being is under primary attack?" Is it the biological drives of my body? If it is, then I know it's Type *C* coming from the flesh. If it is my ego, my pride, then I know it's Type *B* coming from the world. Form the habit of analyzing what kind of temptation you are going through. This sounds awkward but it is crucial. In time, this analysis of each serious temptation can become almost automatic.

We will now go over three temptations in the Bible and try to identify each temptation as to basic type. In Genesis 13:5, 6 we read, "And Lot also, which went with Abram, had flocks, and herds, and tents. And the land was not able to bear them, that they might dwell together: for their substance was great, so that they could not dwell together." As this narrative takes up, Abram and Lot were wealthy cattlemen and because of this they were having trouble finding grazing lands. Now notice the next verse: "And there was a strife between the herdmen of Abram's cattle and the herdmen of Lot's cattle: and the Canaanite and the Perizzite dwelled then in the land." Actually, this is the first recorded range war in history. You could paraphrase this that Abram's cowboys began to fight Lot's cowboys over the range land. The point is that the Canaanite and the Perizzite were looking on as these two men of God were fighting each other. Abram had been commissioned to go to Palestine to be a testimony to Jehovah, and here they were fighting each other. Abram realized that this was a very poor testimony, so he made a very gracious offer. "And Abram said unto Lot, Let there be no strife, I pray thee, between me and thee, and between my herdmen and thy herdmen; for we be brethren. Is not the whole land before thee? separate thyself, I pray thee, from me: if thou wilt take the left hand, then I will go to the right; or if thou depart to the right hand, then I will go to the left" (vs.

8, 9). In other words he says, "Lot, if you want the land over here, I'll take what is left." Abram was obviously concerned about the testimony of God rather than personal gain. Now you have to realize that they were standing on a rise of ground and on one side was the lush, rich, semitropical Jordan Valley. On the other side was what they call in the Bible the "Judean wilderness." When you read that in the Bible you don't want to think of jungle underbrush or baboons swinging through trees on vines. The Judean wilderness is an arid, parched land where a decent lizard would have a hard time surviving.

Now Lot was faced with a decision, "And Lot lifted up his eyes, and beheld all the plain of Jordan, that it was well watered every where, before the Lord destroyed Sodom and Gomorrah, even as the garden of the Lord, like the land of Egypt, as thou comest unto Zoar. Then Lot chose him all the plain of Jordan; and Lot journeyed east: and they separated themselves the one from the other" (vs. 10, 11).

Perhaps you are saying, "Where's the temptation? I don't even see that this fellow was being tempted." But he was. He may not have been doing anything illegal or immoral, but he was being tempted. In fact, this was the greatest temptation that he would ever face. And as a result of this decision here, his spiritual career gets worse. In fact, a few chapters away he loses everything!

Now what prompted him to go into the Jordan valley? Read verse 10 again. "And Lot lifted up his eyes, and beheld all the plain of Jordan, that it was well watered . . . before the Lord destroyed Sodom and Gomorrah." Notice that there were two cities down there in that valley called Sodom and Gomorrah, and we know from the Bible that they were swinging cities. They had their discotheques, their booze, their broads, their topless this and bottomless that, and all the rest of it. But as you read verse 10 is there any indication that that is what Lot was after—getting some of that fast living down in Sodom and Gomorrah? He was obviously enticed by the well-watered grassland. Why did he want grass? Did he eat grass? No! He wanted it for his cattle. Lot wanted to be the biggest cattleman in all of Palestine. He was not concerned with God's glory as was Abram, but with personal gain for ego purposes. So in this instance we are obviously dealing with Type *B* temptation. The *world* was attacking his ego. Perfectly moral and legal things of the world were enticing him.

Now, let's turn to another temptation. In 2 Samuel 11:1, 2 we read, "And it came to pass, after the year was expired, at the time when kings go forth to battle, that David sent Joab, and his servants with him, and all Israel; and they destroyed the children of Ammon, and besieged Rabbah. But David tarried still at Jerusalem. And it came to pass in an eveningtide, that David arose from off his bed, and walked upon the roof of the king's house: and from the roof he saw a woman washing herself; and the woman was very beautiful to look upon." I don't need to continue, you all know this story—the story of David and Bathsheba. Now what is David's problem here? Is his ego under attack? Does he want to be a big shot like Lot? No! Obviously, we are dealing with Type *C;* the appetites of the body were under attack.

For one more instance of biblical temptation, turn to Luke 22:-54-57, the trial of our Lord. Jesus is in the Garden of Gethsemane praying and the soldiers are going to come and get Him and take Him to be tried and then crucified. "Then took they him, and led him, and brought him into the high priest's house. And Peter followed afar off. And when they had kindled a fire in the midst of the hall, and were set down together, Peter sat down among them. But a certain maid beheld him as he sat by the fire, and earnestly looked upon him, and said, This man was also with him. And he denied him, saying, Woman, I know him not."

Now here is Peter's great temptation. Did Peter have the same problem that David had? Did he say, "Oh, that young girl is looking seductively at me?" No! The basic thrust of the temptation was right at his *relationship with God.* He was tempted successfully to deny his Lord. His *God-consciousness* was under primary attack. So, in this instance, we are dealing with Type *A:* Satan attacking his spirit or God-consciousness. Now our analysis has led us to the conclusion that this temptation by its very nature must be coming from direct demonic attack.

To show that we are on the right track, let's look at a remark that Christ made to Peter a few days prior to this incident. Notice what Christ said in Luke 22:31, "And the Lord said, Simon, Simon, behold, Satan hath desired to have you, that he may sift you as wheat." A few days before it happened, Christ said, "Watch out, Peter, the devil is after you." When the devil did attack him, he attacked him right in the area of his God-consciousness.

Now the question is, "How do I handle these different types of temptation?" What does the Bible say to do about it? What are the tactics? I think, numerically, over the period of your life-span, Type *B* will be the most prominent: the world attacking the ego. This is true particularly in our materialistic society. Let's suppose that some of you ladies find yourselves enamored with the latest fashions. You are supposed to look sharp for the glory of God and yet it gets to be more than that. All you can think about are clothes; and you find yourselves constantly reading magazines about the latest fashions. It becomes an inordinate passion that's ever on your mind. Clothes! Clothes! Clothes! How do you handle that? Do you get all of your money together and go down in front of all the pretty dress shops and try to fight it? That would probably be devastating. Or, you fellows get the Dodge fever. Cars! How do we handle it?

If we would just take the time to look into the Word of God once in a while it might help us. In 1 John 2:15 we read, "Love not the world, neither the things that are in the world. If any man love the world, the love of the Father is not in him." His problem is that something has happened to his love for God. If you begin to let your love for God grow cold, then the world will slip into the vacuum. So, if you find yourself loving the world inordinately, that is a *symptom* of a deeper problem. Don't fight the symptom, let the symptom warn you of the real problem, and your real problem is that something has happened to your love for God.

Suppose I'm driving along on the freeway and the green light comes on my dashboard and I say, "Boy, that's bugging me." So I get a hammer and smash it out. That wouldn't solve anything! That green light is warning me of a deeper problem and the problem is in my engine—it needs oil. Just dealing with the symptom doesn't help anything. You should allow the symptom to warn you of the real problem.

When you begin to have an inordinate love for the things of the world, then your real problem is that you are not loving God. Something has happened to that love relationship. The chief issue in successful Christian living is maintaining this love relationship, and if that begins to slip, then all kind of other things take place. One of the things that will take place is that you will begin to love the things of this world: ego, status, clothes, cars, security, and so forth. So let that warn you. Don't fight that temptation, but let that temptation warn you about your lack of love. Check out your devotional life. Get alone with Him and start really having a time with Him. Get that love back where it ought to be and the whole problem will disappear. Because if you love Him as you ought to love Him, you won't be loving this world. The more you love Him, the less important the things of this world will become to you.

I'm sure you have sung about this. So often we sing songs that have fine words, with our minds in neutral. I'm sure you've sung this song that really presents the solution to this problem: "Turn your eyes upon Jesus. Look full in His wonderful face, and the things of earth will grow strangely dim, in the light of His glory and grace." That's exactly what we are talking about. So when you are tempted with Type *B* (the world), check out your devotional life. Check out your communication with Him. Review chapters one and two again. It is absolutely crucial in maintaining a successful Christian life to take time every day to communicate with Him, and that is why a time of daily personal devotions is so important. Because, if you are not really communicating with Him every day in a meaningful way, pretty soon the world will slip into the vacuum and your love will grow cold.

Now let's move to a consideration of Type C: the flesh attacking the appetites of the body. And, of course, the big issue in that type of temptation is sex, particularly in our culture. Pitirim Sorokin called it "the omnipresent sex stimuli!" It's all around us! Sometime when you are sitting in front of the TV just take note of all the different products that are being sold with a sex pitch. It will absolutely amaze you. Everything from toasters to toothpaste, everything from spark plugs to shaving cream are being sold by sex. A fellow is lathering up, and there is sultry music in the background and a Swedish voice comes on, "Take it off, take it all off." How are we to handle this type of temptation?

Teaching at a college, I naturally am called upon to counsel young people with sex temptations. Though we have Christian students, they are very much alive and very normal. Every year I have young fellows come to me and say, "Dr. Mitchell, I've been dating Susy Smith for some weeks now and I'm getting tempted." I say, "What else is new? If you weren't, there would be something wrong with you. You'd better see a doctor." Then the young man responds somewhat as follows: "Well, Dr. Mitchell, we've already decided how we are going to handle it. We have a biology class together so tonight we are going to gather algae off the rocks in Newport Beach. If we get down there and get tempted on that lonely beach, we've already decided what we are going to do. Right on the spot we're going to kneel down and pray and ask God to help us to fight this thing." Now that sounds very pious, but that's very stupid! That's like sticking your head in the lion's mouth and asking God to help it not to bite you. God is very specific as to how you handle that type of temptation.

Every time God talks about it, He uses the same tactics. For instance, take a look at 2 Timothy 2:22, "Flee . . . youthful lusts."

Or, 1 Corinthians 6:18, "Flee fornication." Every time the Bible talks about this, it advises the same tactic. You are never told to fight but to *flee!* Any good general knows when it's time to retreat and when dealing with Type *C,* it's time to retreat. Read about Joseph in Genesis 39. When Potiphar's wife tried to seduce him, did Joseph suggest that they kneel beside the couch and pray about it? No! He ran! He ran so fast he left the old girl holding onto his coat and he did exactly the right thing!

However, there are different ways to run. Sometimes you will have to literally run with your feet as did Joseph. But more often you will be called upon to run from the situation. Now what does that mean? Let me cite a few examples. If young people are having problems then they shouldn't go on dates to a secluded rendez-vous where they are all alone. That's not running. That's asking for it! Rather, they should structure their dates at places with lots of bright lights and lots of people. Go to a baseball or football game on Saturday afternoon with fifty thousand people around. I promise you nothing is going to happen to you in that stadium. You are running from the situation.

Suppose a secretary bats her false eyelashes at her boss and seductively suggests that they meet back at the office that evening to catch up on their work. How should the man handle it? He should agree to meet the sexy secretary and then invite his mother-in-law to accompany him to the office. If he does this, I can assure you that he is running from the situation. Nothing amiss will transpire.

When young people insist on concluding a date with a good-night kiss, I recommend to the fellows not to kiss the young lady goodnight in a back alley—that's not running, that's asking for it. Kiss her goodnight right on the front porch of her home under-neath the porch light with her father looking through the keyhole with a shotgun, and I promise you, you are running!

Now this same tactic is to be used anytime the biological drives are under attack, regardless of whether or not it involves sex. I don't try to fight my appetite for doughnuts or I get clobbered, because God tells me not to fight that type of temptation, but to run! I can't stand there looking at those chocolate éclairs and all of the other goodies without meeting defeat. I end up going in and stuffing myself. I've found it necessary to instruct my wife not to serve my meals family style any longer. I just can't sit at the table with all of those goodies piled in front of me. She now puts my portions on my plate in the kitchen. She places the plate with the proper portions in front of me. I eat it and get away from the table as fast as I can. This is running from the situation.

And by the way, there has been more than one young person whom God has delivered from narcotic addiction and the enemy has tricked him into going back and witnessing to his old friends. That sounds pious, but it's not running! God says to run from it. So what happens; they get hooked again themselves. I've seen that happen more than once. The same thing has happened to people with drinking problems. In both cases, the convert must be advised to run. He must make a clean break with the old environment.

Finally, how does one handle Type A: direct demonic attack upon the God-consciousness? The Bible again is clear. Note if you will the admonition in James 4:7, "Submit yourselves therefore to God. Resist the devil, and he will flee from you." How does one resist the devil? I can think of no better way to resist the devil than the way Jesus Christ handled a direct satanic overture. Each time He used the same tactical maneuver. "It is written." "It is written." "It is written." He hit him over the head with the sword of the Spirit which is the Word of God. He threw Scripture in his teeth. That is the best way to resist the devil.

With Type A temptation we are supposed to resist in the power of the Spirit, but *using the Word of God.* For instance, if Satan tries to tell a new convert that he is not saved, the best thing to do is to have a passage that states categorically that all who believe in Christ have everlasting life. Throw a verse like John 5:24

in the enemy's face. Or if you are tempted to doubt God's good-ness—if some tragedy occurs in your life and you are tempted to "curse God and die," the best thing to do is throw the promises of God in the teeth of the devil.

Thus, to effectively handle this kind of temptation you must *know* your Bible. That is why Scripture memorization is so impor-tant. David said, "Thy word have I hid in mine heart, that I might not sin against thee" (Psalms 119:11). You must really get to know your weapon and how to use it. I'm told that a marine becomes so proficient in using his rifle that he can take it apart and put it back together again blindfolded. When the devil came to Jesus to tempt Him, Christ didn't say, "Now wait a minute, Satan, I've got to go check with my rabbi to see what Scripture to hit you with." No, He knew His Bible. He had mastered it. The more you hide God's Word in your heart, the more you study this Book and master it, the more you will be prepared to deal effectively with this type of temptation.

Now allow me to make a final observation. As a person pro-ceeds chronologically through life, the emphasis in temptations seems to move from *C* to *B* to *A* as noted below.

A. Devil —— Spirit
B. World — Soul
↑ **C. Flesh —— Body** ↑
↑ ↑ ↑ ↑ ↑ ↑ ↑

You will find that with young people, Type *C* is tremendously significant. The bodily drives, particularly sex drives, are very, very sensitive. During middle age, Type *B* becomes more and more prominent. I'm not saying that there will be no temptation from Type *C* anymore, but the middle-aged person becomes increasingly concerned with security, status, Dun and Bradstreet rating, and so forth. In other words, the world (Type *B*) becomes very important. Then, when a person reaches the sunset years of life, there tends to be a decrease in the influence in Types *C* and

B temptations. When a child of God reaches old age the flesh temptations are generally no problem. Not just the sex drives, but even overeating is not a problem. People in rest homes have to be made to eat. It's just a mechanical procedure that they have to go through and usually a nurse practically forces them to eat. These matters pose no problem for a Christian eighty or ninety years of age.

The same thing can be said for Type *B*. Older people have decreasing ego problems. They often don't care how they dress or if their hair is combed or not. Status is no problem, but my how these older Christians are bothered by Type *A*. The enemy seems to be constantly trying to get them to doubt God's Word, doubt His faithfulness and goodness.

I've been a pastor and I know what I'm talking about. That's a real problem for older Christians. Let me assure you that it will make a difference in your older years if you take time to really master the Bible and learn how to handle the Scripture while you are young. It will really pay big dividends, especially in your declining years, because you'll have a reservoir to draw upon when harassed by the enemy.

So, by way of conclusion, when tempted by the devil in the area of your God-consciousness, resist with the Word. When tempted by the world in the area of your ego, check out your devotional love for Him. That's where the real problem lies. When tempted by the flesh, in the biological drives of the body, run, baby, run! Needless to say, all of these tactical maneuvers must be carried out by utilizing the power of the indwelling Holy Spirit!

4

God's Morality Versus the New Morality

I think all will concur that one of the watchwords of current society is *ecology.* Everyone is concerned about pollution: polluting our streams, polluting our air, et cetera. So many people are talking about the pollution of the physical universe, yet hardly any seem to talk about the most serious of all types of pollution, and that is *moral pollution.* Certain entertainers talk a great deal about ecology, and yet they do not seem the least bit concerned about polluting the morals of the people. It's evident that our society is suffering from tremendous moral pollution.

I am persuaded that much of our problem has been caused by a renunciation of moral absolutes. In most colleges and universities today young people are being exposed to the concept of moral relativity. They are assured that there are no such things as absolute moral standards. There was a time not too many years ago in this country when it was felt by virtually everyone that lying was wrong and always wrong. It was held to be almost axiomatic that extramarital or premarital sexual intercourse was always wrong. In short, Americans generally felt that there were absolute standards of right and wrong. Now, I am not saying that thirty years ago all Americans told the truth. However, thirty years ago when Americans lied they were conscious of a moral fault. That is increasingly not true today! It is especially not true among college and university young people because in their ethics classes

63

many are being taught that lying is not always wrong. They are told that lying may be right in certain situations. This concept has largely been championed by Joseph Fletcher in his book *Situation Ethics.* My observation has been that the so-called new morality has all too often ended up being *no morality.* At any rate, Fletcher and the advocates of situation ethics end up by insisting that lying is not always wrong, stealing is not always wrong, extramarital sex is not always wrong. It just depends on the situation. Increasingly, there seem to be no standards of right and wrong. Everybody just makes up his own mind and does his own thing. (For a complete discussion of the pros and cons of situation ethics, let me recommend a book by Fletcher and Montgomery entitled *Situation Ethics,* published by Bethany Fellowship, Minneapolis, Minnesota. It is actually a high-level debate between these two individuals over this issue. Fletcher obviously defends situation ethics and Montgomery effectively repudiates it.)

What is the result of all this? Moral pollution at the grass-roots level! Venereal disease is now in epidemic proportion. Abortions are skyrocketing. Crime and violence are mushrooming. I predict that shortly we will see homosexuality legalized in many parts of our nation.

We ask the question then, "Are morals absolute? Are there no standards of right and wrong? Are we just left to waste away in our own moral excretion?" I want to state categorically that morals are *essentially absolute.* We do have clear, concise moral guidelines given to us. In the remainder of this chapter, three issues will be discussed, namely: the basis of moral absolutes; the character of moral absolutes, and the chief problem with moral absolutes.

The Basis of Moral Absolutes

In order to have moral absolutes, you need two things. First of all we must recognize the existence of an absolute transcendent

God. He must be infinite in righteousness and wisdom. Only such a Being could be in a position to lay down absolute standards of right and wrong for mankind. Certainly no finite man could ever be capable of laying down such rules. This entire planet is about the size of a grain of sand in the vast universe. Men are like microscopic particles crawling around on this grain of sand. None of us from such a perspective are in a position to know what is absolutely right or wrong for society, individually or collectively. Our experience is too limited. We are simply not smart enough. The relegation of moral absolutes demands somebody outside the system, who is beyond the system, who can see the big picture, who has infinite wisdom. Such a Being alone is in a position to lay down moral absolutes. There must be an absolute God!

It just so happens that I believe that we do have precisely this kind of a God. Isaiah saw the Lord high and lifted up, and the angels gathered round about the throne weren't singing, "Shall we gather at the river," or "Love lifted me"; they were singing, "Holy, holy, holy is the Lord God Almighty!" (see Isaiah 6:1-3). The God of the universe is a moral Being and this is a moral universe. Therefore, we *do* have an absolutely holy God who is in a position to really legislate moral absolutes.

Now, not only must we have the existence of an infinite moral God, but this God must reveal His absolute standards to men. In short, we must have an absolute *revelation* from God. If God simply existed and never revealed to men in clear-cut terms what is right and what is wrong, we still could not have moral absolutes. You must not only have the existence of an absolute God, but an absolute record from that God. Again, I believe that this is exactly what we have in the Bible. (I am assuming that my reader is convinced of the complete infallibility of the Holy Scriptures. For those who would like a more detailed discussion of this matter, let me suggest a fine little work entitled: *Can I Trust My Bible,* edited by Howard F. Vos, Moody Press.)

The Bible is a written permanent record of the outbreathing of

God; and when God in the Bible clearly says something is right, it's right and always right for one reason: because an absolute God says so! When God, in the Bible, clearly says something is wrong, it's wrong and always wrong. That means wrong for anybody at any time or under any circumstances for one reason, and that is because *God says so!* Right and wrong are not what man thinks, but what God says. God dictates ethics; little man does not. If God in the Bible says certain things are clearly right and certain things are clearly wrong with no limitations, then, brother, they are *absolutes.*

If you deny either one of these two assumptions, moral absolutes are impossible. So in theological language, the two assumptions necessary for moral absolutes are: theism, the existence of an absolute God; and, inspiration; God has revealed an infallible record of His mind and will. If a man denies theism and inspiration, he must ultimately deny moral absolutes. Destroy God and the Bible and you have no adequate basis for morality. To illustrate this point, some years ago, a board of education finally decided that they had better start teaching morals in the public schools. For years all moral instruction had been virtually outlawed in public education in that state. Public-school teachers were not allowed to teach morals. As a result, they were beginning to turn out monsters, so they decided that they had better start teaching some rudimentary ethical values. However, once they decided to teach morals, they had to decide upon a proper basis for such moral values. Upon what basis does one tell little Willie and little Mary, "You're supposed to tell the truth. You can't lie!" Who says so? On what basis? They couldn't say, "Because God in the Bible tells you you shouldn't lie," because for years public education has all too often led in a seemingly systematic attempt to discredit the Bible as the authoritative Word of God. Well, they wrestled with this problem for hours. What basis could they give for the moral values they wanted taught in public schools? Finally, the only thing they could come up with was "Traditional Americanism." "Little

Willie and little Mary, you shouldn't lie because Americans tradi-
tionally have not lied!" Now if there is anything that will *not*
appeal to today's youth, it is something like that! Yet, that is the
best they could do. You destroy God and the Bible, and you
destroy the basis for effective morality among a free people.

The Explicitness of Moral Absolutes

Having shown that in God and the Bible we have an adequate
basis for moral absolutes, let us next ask the question, "Does the
Bible lay down clear moral absolutes?" I believe that a careful
study of the Scriptures will reveal that the Bible is filled with clear,
precise moral absolutes. God has given us a great deal of information as to what is right and what is wrong. For example, in the Ten
Commandments we find clear moral guidelines from God to the
nation Israel. In the New Testament nine of these commands are
repeated almost word for word. God says that adultery is wrong.
It's always wrong. Regardless of the culture, it is always wrong.
God says lying is wrong, and always wrong. These are absolutes,
because God without any limitations has said that they are wrong.
In Proverbs 6:16-19, you read about seven deadly sins: "These
six things doth the Lord hate: yea, seven. . . ." Now these things
are always wrong. I don't care if they are committed by a Fiji
Islander or a fellow in America, it's always wrong because God
says so. In the New Testament we have Jesus in the Sermon on
the Mount (Matthew 5-7) giving many clear moral guidelines. In
the Epistles there are also numerous passages giving detailed ethical instruction (Romans 1:28-32; 1 Thessalonians 5:11-26; Galatians 5:18-23, et cetera). Yes, the Bible gives us much by way of
clear moral guidelines and many of them are stated in absolute
universal terms with no evident qualifications. When God clearly
says that something is right, it's always right and absolutely right.
When God says something is wrong, it's wrong and always wrong
and absolutely wrong *because God says so*. To be sure, there are

instances in the Bible where men violated God's clear commands. Abraham lied, but that doesn't mean that God condoned it! Lying is always wrong. Kindness is always right. Therefore, the Bible does contain clear, explicit moral absolutes.

Now let me also add this. When stated in an unqualified manner, the moral guidelines of the Bible are not only *absolute* but they are *good* for man. You will find that God's laws are good for society and good for you! I have known people who are atheists and yet they pretty generally followed the moral guidelines of the Bible. Why? Because they have discovered that this is the good way to live. I read an article on Castro's Cuba some time ago and it brought out the fact that they do not have any adultery in Cuba. Why? Because Castro shoots adulterers! Now why does Castro do that? Does he love God? No! Castro has discovered that it is not good for his people. You will find that God knows what is good for mankind to a far greater extent then some sociologist who has always lived in his academic ivory tower! Ultimately, only God knows what is really good for society. The rest of us are giving educated guesses at best. Let them argue all they want about the legitimacy of homosexual conduct. God says that it is an abomination and that it will destroy a society! Frankly, I'm going to put my money with God.

Problems With Biblical Ethics

Let us now consider several practical problems encountered by Christians in the area of ethics. There is a tremendous need among the people of God to get back to the morals of the Bible. I think that we as Christians are guilty of "straining at gnats and swallowing camels" (*see* Matthew 23:24). We have reduced ethical standards to a few objective taboos, and so long as we don't drink a can of beer or suck on a cigarette, we consider ourselves moral. We scrupulously avoid these few externals, but we pay no attention to pride, backbiting, gossip, and the like. For example: I dare say for most evangelical Christian young people, the thought of drinking a can of beer would be simply horrifying! Yet, they would think nothing of smarting off to their parents. I want to tell you something. Drinking a can of beer is peanuts compared to being disrespectful to your parents! We need to get back to what the Bible really talks about. I'm not saying that we should eat gnats. It's not good to eat gnats, but let's take care of these camels. Let me give another illustration. Usually when we think of a carnal Christian we think of some fellow who still hasn't kicked the cigarette habit or plays with the wrong kind of playing cards or gambles. Yet, Paul gives a clear statement about carnality. He states: ". . . ye are yet carnal: for . . . there is among you envying, and strife, and divisions" (1 Corinthians 3:3). My, but Paul certainly had a funny concept of sin. He missed all the big ones! He said nothing about bottle-blond hair, movies, or dancing. He just mentioned little matters like envy, strife, and divisions! Most Christians take these things almost as a matter of course, yet these are big in the Scriptures. There is nothing more serious than causing discord among the brethren. Read the Epistles of Paul. He constantly stressed the necessity of keeping unity among believers (Ephesians 4:1-3, Philippians 2:1-4, Colossians 3:12-14). Yet often we think a good church fight is almost routine. To be at odds with another Christian is a terrible thing in the Scripture. Yes, we need to get back to the morality of the Bible. We've neglected the weightier matters of the law.

Time and time again the Scriptures warn believers not to be conformed to this world, yet the average Christian thinks that so long as he doesn't participate in a certain set of so-called worldly amusements, he is following God's admonition. We're not worldly because we don't go to horse races, or honky-tonks, yet we can be materialistic to the core and take on this world's value system. A careful study of worldliness will reveal much broader concepts than most Christians realize. Let me say it again. We need to get back to the ethics of the old Book. The average

Christian knows far more about what Dear Abby says about morals than what the Bible says about them, because they read Dear Abby far more faithfully and consistently. We need to get back to the Book and find out what it really says about morality.

The more you determine to set your ethical standards by the Bible, the more you can expect to be out of step with society around you. You may even be misunderstood by other Christians. Fifty years ago traditional American values and biblical values were pretty much alike—at least far closer than they are today. Over the years there has been a greater and greater gap between biblical values and traditional American values. In the last ten years American ethical values have deteriorated at an alarming rate. Now as they deteriorate the gap gets wider. If you are following biblical standards and everybody else is following deteriorated American standards, you are bound to be misunderstood. You are going to be considered an oddball. Indeed, the day may soon come when you might even be considered an enemy of society. Have you read *Brave New World?* It pictures a future day when society will consider people who live together as husband and wife as evil oddities. So, you can expect to be more and more out of step and misunderstood. We are approaching the day when black is being called white, and vice versa.

Yet by far the greatest problem faced by Christians in the area of ethics is in those areas where God *does not* speak clearly. How do we gauge our ethical conduct in the areas where the Bible is not clear? If you can, imagine the things that God clearly says are right as a white area, and the things that God clearly says are wrong as a black area. Most Christians are not troubled so much with the white or the black. However, when the white and black come together there is not a sharp line of demarcation. There is kind of a dirty gray area. You don't know whether something is right or wrong because the Bible doesn't clearly say. How do we conduct ourselves in this area? For instance, I never find a statement in the Bible saying, "Thou shalt watch Lawrence Welk on

TV, or thou shalt not watch Lawrence Welk on TV." As a sincere Christian, how do I know whether or not I should watch the program?

By the way, why shouldn't I expect to find a statement like that in the Bible? What would that kind of statement mean to most of the people in the world today? Nothing! What would it mean to us thirty years from now? Nothing! We must realize that the Bible wasn't written just for people who live in the United States now. It was written for all people in all periods of history. Therefore, we can't expect to find detailed information on all aspects of our culture.

What is the solution? The solution to this type of ethical problem is that the Bible gives us *broad principles* which we can apply to matters like watching Lawrence Welk on TV. Whatever ethical question you might have, if you will honestly apply these biblical principles you can know what you should do.

Now, before we go into the actual principles themselves, I want to give a few ground rules for applying the biblical principles. Do not confuse these so-called ground rules with the principles themselves. *The first ground rule is to apply these principles personally.* Don't try to apply them to your friends. What do I mean by this? By way of example, let's say that you study the biblical principles and decide that you should not watch Lawrence Welk on TV. That's fine, but don't turn around and tell me not to watch it! You apply the principles for yourself. The Bible is very clear that in the area of doubtful things each Christian is to decide honestly before the Lord what he is supposed to do and not try to tell other people what they should do. Each person is to decide for himself (*see* Romans 14:1-6), so apply these biblical principles personally.

The second ground rule can be stated as follows: *Just because the Bible doesn't explicitly forbid a thing doesn't mean that it is necessarily the right thing to do.* I've had many people, over the years, say, "Well, the Bible doesn't say it's wrong." They then conclude illogically that it must be right. This is not a safe assumption. Does anybody know any place in the Bible where it says, "Thou shalt not inject heroin into thy veins"? It's not there, but does that mean it's right? No! It's not safe to say that something is right just because the Bible doesn't explicitly forbid it.

Third, *just because you think it's okay doesn't mean that it is the proper course of action to take.* How often have you heard Christians say, "Well, I don't see anything wrong with it," and then they proceed on that basis to go ahead and do it. We are going to see that there is more to consider than your own personal opinion.

Now another thing. *Just because it's fun, doesn't mean that it is sinful.* Some Christians seem to have the idea that anything that is fun must be sinful. In the early days of colonial America, an English minister visited this new nation. Following the Sunday morning service someone invited him home for dinner. When it came time for dessert, they asked the minister if he would like to try a new colonial delicacy—ice cream. The minister agreed to try a dish, but upon taking the first spoonful he pushed it aside. The hostess said, "Reverend, what is wrong? Don't you like it? To which the minister replied, "It was delicious!" Quite naturally the hostess asked, "Well, why don't you eat it?" He replied, "Anything that good must be sinful." Some of us think this way! Do not allow yourself to fall into that trap.

A fifth ground rule is that *in the area of doubtful things, morals can be relative.* We have already made quite a point that ethics are essentially absolute. When God gives clear, detailed, absolute moral instructions in unqualified terms these are absolute. However, in those areas where the Bible is silent or is not clear, morals can be relative. In everyday language what I am saying is that it is possible for two Christians to be doing identically the same thing at the same time and one to be sinning and the other not. I know that this sounds strange, but you will see how this is possible before we finish this chapter. Again, we are not saying that all morals are relative, only that they can be relative in the area of doubtful things.

One final ground rule is that *you must be honest in the application of biblical principles.* This is beyond question the most important ground rule. The principles we are about to discuss will be a safe guide for your ethical conduct if you will honestly apply them. If you are not honest, they will not work. Human nature tends to justify itself. All too often when we want to do something bad enough it's hard to be really honest. So you must really make a concentrated effort to be honest in the application of these principles.

Now let's move into a consideration of the actual biblical principles. I will discuss five principles. Four of the five will be from one book in the Bible. This is for convenience and does not mean that this one book is the only place where these principles can be found in Scripture. The first principle is stated in 1 Corinthians 10:23: "All things are lawful for me, but all things are not expedient: all things are lawful for me, but all things edify not." I realize that the primary reference is to dietary regulations, but it is not out of harmony with the thrust of the Bible to make a broader application. For a Christian there is more to be considered than the legality of a matter. Just because a thing is legal doesn't mean that it is right. I have already predicted that we will see the day when homosexual conduct will be legalized in many parts of our nation. If this happens, that will not make it right. A legal decision is not always a moral decision. As a Christian I must consider more than the legality of a matter. Paul says, "All things edify not." The implication is that I should engage in activity that edifies. What does the word *edify* mean? It's an old English word that means "to build up." I should endeavor to do those things that build me up physically, morally, and spiritually. I should participate in things that make me a more wholesome individual. There are some foods that you can eat which will definitely build you up. There are other foods that will definitely be harmful to your body. There are certain books you can read that will definitely make you a more wholesome individual. There are other books which you can read that will definitely tear you down. This principle can have wide application. I believe that everything has a tendency to build up or tear down. So you should ask yourself, "Does this make me a more wholesome individual? Does it build me up or tear me down?" The first principle then is, *"Does it build?"*

Another principle is found in the eighth chapter of 1 Corinthians. Paul begins this chapter with the words, "Now as touching things offered unto idols. . . ." Evidently the early believers at Corinth had a problem and they wrote to the Apostle Paul to seek his advice concerning the matter. In Corinth there existed but one little group of believers. On the street corners of their city were various pagan temples rather than churches. Now, it was the custom in Corinth for the pagans to bring meat and offer it in sacrifice to idols. They would bring in a rib roast, hamburger or T-bone steak, and lay it before the idol. After making some incantations they would leave. The pagan priest would come in, take the meat that had been offered to the idol, slip it out the back door and offer it for sale in the supermarket at half price.

Now here is the ethical problem that these early Christians faced. Is it right for me to take advantage of this bargain at the supermarket? Should I buy meat that has been offered to a pagan idol? Not knowing exactly what to do, they wrote Paul and asked him about the matter. Now I have never personally had this ethical problem. In fact, I dare say that none of you have had the problem either. However, the interesting thing is that Paul didn't write back and say, "Naughty, naughty, you can't eat it." Nor does he write back and tell them to go ahead and eat it. What he does do is give them a principle and tells them to honestly apply that principle and then decide for themselves. The beautiful thing is that I can take the principle he gave them and apply it to the things that bother me in my culture.

What did Paul tell them? Basically he says, "Now look folks, we know that that idol is just a piece of rock and that there is nothing evil in the actual idol. So if you lay a perfectly good T-bone steak down in front of the idol there is nothing that emanates out of it that will put the whammy on the meat. There is nothing wrong with the meat. You are not any better if you eat it and no worse if you don't. It's no question of the meat at all." Paul sums the whole matter up with these words, "But meat commendeth us not to God: for neither, if we eat, are we the better; neither, if we eat not, are we the worse" (1 Corinthians 8:8). Knowledge says there is nothing wrong in eating the meat, but Paul is quick to point out that there is more to be considered then what knowledge dictates. *Love* must be considered. In verse 9 he says, "But take heed lest by any means this liberty of yours become a stumblingblock to them that are weak." That is love speaking. You see, it's not just a question of what I think about the matter. I must consider how my actions will affect others, especially my Christian brothers. So Paul sums up the whole issue in verse 13, "Wherefore, if meat make my brother to offend, I will eat no flesh while the world standeth, lest I make my brother to offend."

The principle here is, *"Does it cause others to stumble?"* You must not only think what you consider about the matter, but you must consider how your actions will affect your brothers and sisters in Christ. Will it harm them? Will it take away from their spiritual development? Someone is probably saying, "The heck with the other guy. If I don't see anything wrong with it, I am going to go ahead and do it." Such a statement reminds me more of the words of Cain, the first murderer, when he said, "Am I my brother's keeper?" (Genesis 4:9). May I say that the categorical Christian answer to Cain's question is, yes, you are your brother's keeper. That's what love is all about. It's really caring about the other fellow. Did Jesus Christ go around with the attitude, "I don't care what happens to the other guy, I'm going to do whatever I want?" No! So knowledge may say, "There is nothing wrong with it," but love says, "I must consider how my actions affect my brother."

A number of years ago one of my colleagues went down into the southern part of the United States to pursue his education.

While there he obtained a position in a local church as a youth minister. He thought it would be a good recreational activity to take the young people swimming. He loaded them into a bus, drove down to a lake, and they had a great time swimming together. When he returned to the church, the deacons were just about ready to throw him out. Why? Because in that part of the country, at that time, it was considered a terrible sin for boys and girls to go swimming together in the same swimming pool at the same time. It was termed "mixed bathing." The whole matter was new to my friend. He had never heard of such a concept. He saw nothing at all wrong with mixed bathing. He could have said, "Why, these ridiculous people! If I want to go swimming with the girls, I'll go swimming with the girls. I don't see anything wrong with it." That might have been *knowledge,* but *love* said, "If swimming in a mixed situation is going to cause my Christian brothers to stumble and even hurt my testimony for Jesus Christ in this community, then even though I don't see anything wrong with it, I'll not go swimming with the girls. At least I won't until I get back to Southern California. Then I'll go swimming with the girls." I believe that biblically he did exactly the right thing.

So, to be specific, if the Holy Spirit makes it plain to you that something in your conduct is detrimental to your Christian brother, consider that to be God's red light for you. Back off and refrain because you love your brother. Submit because you are concerned about his welfare. Now that doesn't mean you are to go around looking for things in your conduct that might be offensive to others, but if the Spirit of God makes it plain to you, then abstain if it will help your brother.

The third principle is presented in 1 Corinthians 6:12: "All things are lawful unto me, but all things are not expedient: all things are lawful for me, but I will not be brought under the power of any [or anything]." I realize that this statement is in old-fashioned King James English, but what is it saying? It is saying literally, "I will not be a slave to anything." But let me give it to you in twentieth-century American slanguage: "Is it habit forming? Will it make me an addict?" I should not allow anything to make me a slave or an addict. Remember at the outset of our discussion I said that just because the Bible doesn't condemn something doesn't necessarily mean it's right. You never find a categorical statement in the Bible telling you, "Thou shalt not inject heroin into thy veins," but if you really apply this principle you will never fool with the stuff because you can't play around it without becoming an addict.

At this point most Christians think in terms of the fellow that still smokes cigarettes or drinks alcohol. When a minister speaks on this issue everybody mentally zeros in on the poor fellow who still has the cigarette habit. They think, "I sure hope that cigarette sucker is getting this!" The poor chap feels like everybody is ganging up on him, but some of the people who look down their noses at him can't face the day without three cups of coffee. I want you to notice the passage says *anything.* Some of us can't really survive without a case of Cokes a day. It says *anything!* I don't want to be misunderstood, I am not saying that you can't drink Cokes or coffee. The fact is I had a cup with my dinner tonight. I want you to understand, of course, that I can quit anytime I want to. Seriously, I am not trying to act like a disgustingly superpious individual, but if I detected in the slightest that I could not really face the day without a cup of coffee, I personally would feel convicted on the basis of this principle. I would remind you, however, that this principle does not pertain only to things that you shove in your mouth. It says *anything!* Perhaps some of you are addicted to the "boob tube." Do you know that the average American watches that stupid thing six and a half hours a day? If this trend continues, future generations will have eyes like cantalopes and brains like peanuts. Many Christians "don't have time" for their daily Bible reading; they "don't have time" to work on their Sunday-school lesson; they "don't have time" to go out and do church visitation; but brother, they've got time for TV! The preacher had better close his Sunday morning service early enough for them to get home and watch the football game or he's in real trouble.

You can be addicted to good things, too. I knew a young man one time who became addicted to sports. He was a sports nut. He was playing on the church softball team. When he wasn't playing for the church team, he was playing for his company team. When he wasn't playing for his church or company, he was up watching the Los Angeles Dodgers play. He was neglecting his wife; he was neglecting his young baby; he was neglecting his responsibilities to the Lord. He was hopelessly addicted to sports. Now, fortunately, the story has a happy ending. He is now a minister in Southern California; but before God could effectively use him, he had to acknowledge the thing for what it really was —sin!

For the next principle we must leave the Book of 1 Corinthians and move into the Book of Romans. In Romans 14:21 Paul says, "It is good neither to eat flesh, nor to drink wine, nor any thing whereby thy brother stumbleth, or is offended, or is made weak." As you probably realize, we have already seen that principle earlier in 1 Corinthians, and here the apostle repeats it again. Paul continues by saying, "Hast thou faith? have it to thyself before God. Happy is he that condemneth not himself in that thing which he alloweth. And he that doubteth is damned [or reproved] if he eat, because he eateth not of faith: for whatsoever is not of faith is sin" (vs. 22, 23). The final sentence is the principle we want to consider. *"For whatsoever is not of faith is sin."* What is faith? Faith is trust. Faith is confidence. Any time that you are not able to proceed with confidence, when there are serious doubts in your mind, then that is God's red light for you to back off until and unless you can proceed with confidence.

Because of this principle it is possible for two Christians to be doing the same thing at the same time and for one to be sinning and the other not. Let's assume that a young man moves to

Southern California from an area where mixed bathing is considered to be a terrible sin. All of his life he has been taught that
mixed bathing is wrong. He attends a local evangelical church,
and the youth leader stands up and announces that they are going
to have a swimming party at the beach. They load a hundred
young people on buses and take them down to the beach. Ninety-
nine of those young people charge into the surf in full confidence.
It never even enters their minds that anything could be wrong, but
here is the young fellow from the South. All of his life he has been
taught that this is a terrible sin. His heart is pounding. For him to
proceed at that time would be sin, "for whatsoever is not of faith
is sin." Whenever you have serious doubts about a matter consider that God's red light. Back off and never proceed until and
unless you can proceed with confidence.

Perhaps some of you are saying at this point, "This is getting a
little complicated. You mean before I can ever make another
ethical decision about doubtful things I must go through this routine and ask myself if it builds me up or tears me down; if it causes
others to stumble; is it addictive; does it cause me to have serious
doubts?" Let me give you one final principle. I really think it is the
supreme principle. If you forget any or all of the previous four, this
final one alone will always be a safe guide for your ethical conduct
in doubtful things. The principle is stated in 1 Corinthians 10:31,
"Whether therefore ye eat, or drink, or whatsoever ye do, do all
to the glory of God."The principle covers a broad area. "Whatsoever ye do." Can you think of anything that it would not include?
Everything I do is to be done to the glory of God. The principle
is, *"Does it glorify God?"* Now this is kind of a fancy King James
way of putting it. What does it mean in plain everyday English?
I think a good contemporary way of stating this truth would be to
phrase it this way: "Does it make God look good? Does it enhance
the reputation of God? By my doing this, by my engaging in this
conduct, will it make God look good or bad?" Do you understand
that you are an official representative of God? As a Christian you

are representing God all of the time. Everything you do at home, in the office, or on your campus reflects either favorably or unfavorably upon God. You say, "Wait a minute. I appreciate the fact that I'm saved and that my sins are forgiven and I'm going to heaven, but to be a representative of Jesus Christ at all times is an awesome responsibility. I don't want that responsibility!" My friend, the scriptural fact is that you *do have it.* The moment you accepted Jesus Christ you became an ambassador of Christ (*see* 2 Corinthians 5:20). It's a package deal.

In 1972 I traveled in Egypt, Palestine, Turkey, Rome, and Greece. In a very real sense I represented all Americans. If I go to a foreign country and act like a complete idiot, it makes all Americans look bad. If I go over there and conduct myself properly, it reflects favorably on all Americans. It makes all Americans look good. You are a representative of Jesus Christ. So if you are thinking about doing something and the Bible isn't clear as to whether or not you should do it, ask yourself, "How does this make Jesus Christ look?" If you can honestly say it will make Him look good, then proceed. I honestly believe that the application of this one principle alone will always be a safe guide to your conduct in doubtful things.

If you will honestly apply these principles, they will be safe guides and you can know what you should do in any given ethical situation where the Bible is silent. May I remind you again that you must be honest. If you are not honest in the application of these principles, they will not be a safe guide.

Christianity is more than good ethics. Christianity is more than just turning over a *new leaf.* It is receiving a *new life* from God. By reading this chapter a person may have gained the impression that Christianity is simply an ethical system. If that is all it is, I wouldn't be nearly so enthusiastic about it. Over twenty years ago I received Jesus Christ into my heart and life in a simple and yet personal way. When I did this, He radically changed my life. He gave me new goals and new purposes. Over these last twenty years I have seen Jesus Christ change all kinds of people.

If you have been reading this book and have never experienced the transforming power of Christ in your life, why not acknowledge Him now as your Saviour?

5

God's Mental Health Program

One of the really important areas of daily living is our *thought life.* Sad to say, most Christians do not realize this. In fact, I am persuaded that mental hygiene is one of the great neglected areas in evangelical Christian circles. It seems we have almost given up this whole field to the psychologists and psychiatrists. Usually when a minister broaches the area of mental health it is as a theological liberal. Those efforts that have been made are very seldom systematic attempts to determine what the Bible has to say on the thought life. Very few conservative ministers, men who really believe that the Bible is fully inspired, have ever spoken or written on the subject so far as I know. (Naturally there have been exceptions. One such was a fine article on the thought life that came to this writer's attention some fifteen years ago and served to stimulate his own thinking in this area. The article was by Dr. Robert Cook in his book *It's Tough to Be a Teenager.*) Though mental hygiene is a greatly neglected area, it is a very *important* area.

With the advent of modern psychology, we have learned the tremendous significance of the thought life in determining who we are and what we are becoming. We are learning that a person can literally think his way to success or failure. You think about something hard enough and long enough and you are just liable to do it. The amazing thing to me is that the Bible has been saying this for thousands of years. Long before Freud made the scene, the Bible was informing us of the tremendous importance of the thought life.

A few statements will demonstrate what the Bible has always said on this issue. For example, Proverbs 23:7: "For as he thinketh in his heart, so is he." Keep in mind that the Bible uses the word *heart* in a sense of "the heart of the matter," or "the core of man's being." Out of this core of being emanates man's mental activity, emotions, and feelings. As you really contemplate this biblical statement, it becomes apparent that a man is very much a product of his thought life. Look at Proverbs 4:23: "Keep thy heart with all diligence; for out of it are the issues of life." Out of your thought life are the issues of life. It's like a rudder on a ship. A rudder on a ship is a very small part of the total bulk of the ship, and yet the direction of the rudder determines the direction of the entire ship. When the rudder turns, the whole ship turns! By the same token, your thoughts determine the direction of your life. You've heard of that statement, "You are what you eat." I think it would be more accurate to say, "You are what you think!" You are going to be a product of what goes on between your ears. Thus by direct statement the Bible makes it clear that the thought life is of monumental import.

Not only does the Bible directly state that the thought life is crucial, it also insists that the thought life is the *source of our actions!* What you say with your mouth, what you do with your hands, where you go with your feet, really begins between your ears. These things are simply a reflection of what is going on in your mind. In Matthew 12:34 Christ said, "O generation of vipers, how can ye, being evil, speak good things? for out of the abundance of the heart the mouth speaketh." What you say with your mouth is actually out of the abundance of your heart—what goes on in your thought life. Then in Matthew 15:18, 19 Christ made it even stronger when He said, ". . . those things which proceed out of the mouth come forth from the heart; and they defile the man. For out of the heart proceed evil thoughts, murders, adulteries, fornications, thefts, false witness, blasphemies." Not only thoughts, but also actions emanate from man's mental machinery. So, if the Bible is right, you can never control what you do and what you say until you begin to discipline your thoughts! To try to control your actions and your words apart from your thoughts is like trying to put pancake makeup on a cancer. You will never stop it that way. You must get down to the source of the problem.

Years ago my daughter discovered that it did no good to weed devil grass by pulling up only what could be seen on the surface. She soon learned that such a procedure didn't solve the problem at all. To effectively root out devil grass, one must dig beneath the surface down to the roots and get them out. Often we do the same thing! We try to curb our actions and our words without ever paying any attention to our thought life. It is absolutely hopeless. It's like trying to keep the lid on a boiling pot by applying external pressure to the top of the lid! Until someone turns off the fire beneath the pot, it will continue to build up steam and eventually blow. The source of your actions is in the fire of your mind, and that is where your actions must be controlled.

The Bible gives yet another reason for the crucial importance of our thoughts. Do you realize that God is going to judge you in this area? God is going to look over your mental activities some day at the judgment seat of Christ! Listen to the words of 1 Corinthians 4:3-5: "But with me it is a very small thing that I should be judged of you, or of man's judgment: yea, I judge not mine own self. For I know nothing by myself; yet am I not hereby justified: but he that judgeth me is the Lord. Therefore judge nothing before the time, until the Lord come, who both will bring to light the hidden things of darkness, and will make manifest the counsels of the hearts." So God is going to judge and evaluate us not merely on what we say and do, but on what we think! This is a sobering concept, to say the least.

I trust that by this time you can see that you will never be the type of person you want to be until you learn to discipline your mind. But, is it possible to discipline the mind? I honestly believe that the average evangelical believer would answer, "Heavens no! I have enough trouble controlling what my mouth says and where my feet go. I can't possibly worry about what goes on in my mind." I hope we have learned by this time the fallacy of such a statement. It is hopeless to try to control what your mouth says and where your feet go without disciplining the mind.

However, a little reflection will reveal that *it is possible* to discipline the mind. The mind can be disciplined completely on the basis of the natural, apart from the indwelling Holy Spirit. Think, for instance, of Communist brainwashing techniques. These are nothing more than successful attempts at mental discipline. Thought control, if you please. There are Buddhist monks and nuns who have so disciplined their minds that they can concentrate on a given subject for hours without ever wavering. Now, they have done so without the indwelling power of the Holy Spirit. There are also mystics on record who have been able to stop their heartbeat and restart it again by sheer mental effort! Therefore, we can say that even from the perspective of the natural, it is possible to discipline the mind. All of this is aside from any consideration of the Holy Spirit who indwells all believers.

Not only is mental discipline possible, but God *commands* it! Notice, if you will, Philippians 4:8: "Finally, brethren, whatsoever things are true, whatsoever things are honest, whatsoever things are just, whatsoever things are pure, whatsoever things are lovely, whatsoever things are of good report; if there be any virtue, and if there be any praise, think on these things." I would remind you that the statement, "think on these things" is an imperative in the original. That means it is a command. Just as God commands you to be filled with the Spirit and preach the gospel to every creature, He also commands you to discipline your mind. I would also like to point out that this command is in the present tense. This indicates continuous action—"Continuously think on these things." Continuously discipline your mind.

Evidently the Apostle Paul had a very definite goal for his mental discipline, and because Paul said to follow him as he followed Christ (1 Corinthians 11:1), Paul's goal becomes our goal. Just as Paul had a goal for his conduct and other areas of life, he had a definite mental-hygiene goal. We find it stated in 2 Corinthians 10:5: "Casting down imaginations [literally 'reasonings'], and every high thing that exalteth itself against the knowledge of God, and bringing into captivity every thought to the obedience of Christ." Paul's goal was to so discipline his mind that every thought was brought down and made subject to Christ. He so desired to control his thoughts to the point where his total mental activity was in obedience and conformity to Jesus Christ.

Now, just like other spiritual goals in the New Testament, it's rather high, isn't it? But isn't the New Testament filled with high and lofty goals? Are we not urged with Paul to aspire to the very perfection of Jesus Christ? This indeed is the highest of goals. Did Paul ever in his life obtain this goal? No, yet Paul relentlessly pressed toward it (see Philippians 3:12-14). He refused to be satisfied with anything less. The ultimate goal of every Christian is the perfection of Jesus Christ. We will be satisfied with nothing less and yet we know that we will never really completely attain it. At the same time, there is something in us that makes us constantly strive for this perfection. The athlete must always strive to play the perfect game; the artist must always try to paint the perfect picture; the writer must always make an effort to write the perfect piece of literature. So there is in the Christian life a *blessed dissatisfaction!* With reference to our mental activity, our goal is to discipline our minds so that every thought is brought under obedience to Christ. An impossible goal in this life, yet we will be satisfied with nothing less. Hopefully we can and will make progress toward it, and be joyful in the very challenge involved.

You will find that when God lays down a command He will usually give us a method by which it may be carried out if we will only search His Word. I am going to suggest a mental-health program right from Scripture. (This is directed to the *average*

Christian. Christians with severe emotional difficulties are not in view. Such believers would do well to seek specialized help from a competent Christian counselor.) The passage I have in mind is a familiar verse but most people have never thought of it in terms of mental hygiene. Yet, it definitely deals with the subject. Take a look at Romans 12: 1, 2: "I beseech you therefore, brethren, by the mercies of God, that ye present your bodies a living sacrifice, holy, acceptable unto God, which is your reasonable service. And be not conformed to this world: but be ye transformed by the renewing of your mind. . . ." The word *present* carries the idea of turning yourself over to another. We are by decisive action to present our bodies to Him. Your "body" in this statement involves your total person. It is everything that constitutes *you* and that includes your mental machinery.

In these verses the statement "present your bodies" alone is in the active voice. This means that the only thing that God is telling the believer to do is to present *his* body. The crucial thing for you is total faith commitment—deliberate, decisive. The verbs "be not conformed . . . be yet transformed" are passive rather than active. You are not told to conform to the world, rather you are told not to let the world conform you. You are not told to transform your mind, rather you are told to allow the Holy Spirit to transform you. The difference between an active and passive verb is that in an active verb the subject is acting, while in the passive verb the subject is being acted upon. For instance, in the statement, "Johnny threw the ball," Johnny is the subject and the subject is doing something. However, in the statement, "The ball was thrown by Johnny," we have an example of a passive verb. The subject of this sentence is the ball. The ball is not doing anything. The ball is having something done to it. Now both verbs in verse 2 are passive, thus in the verse, Paul is telling us what will happen if we make the decisive commitment of verse one. Namely, we will thereby not be allowing the world to conform us, but rather will be allowing the Holy Spirit to transform us. We have two possibilities each day. Either the world is conforming us, or the Holy Spirit is transforming us. If you are in the state of commitment advocated in verse 1, you will be transformed. If you are not in the state of commitment, the world will be conforming you. It is one or the other—conformation or transformation.

I would remind you that these verbs do not convey the thought of *instantaneous* action. They are present tense verbs conveying *continuous* action. Gradually each day the world is conforming you, or the Holy Spirit is transforming you. If you are presenting your body as a living sacrifice, then you are not being gradually conformed by this world. You are being transformed. If you are not presenting your bodies as a living sacrifice, then you are not being gradually transformed, you are being conformed. It is God's desire that you be transformed rather than conformed. The word *transformed* carries the idea of metamorphosis. It is what happens to a caterpillar that crawls into a cocoon and comes out a beautiful butterfly. That's metamorphosis! God wants to metamorphize you!

Now, how does the indwelling Holy Spirit transform you? The text says that it is done "by the renewing of your mind." The Holy Spirit transforms you gradually and He starts with your mental machinery. Is this not the logical place for Him to start? After all, as we have seen previously, what you think is going to determine what you are. So gradually our minds are renewed. The word translated *renew* means to "make new." Your mind needs an overhaul job; but notice carefully, you are not called upon to overhaul it. You are supposed to present the whole self to God and allow Him to overhaul your mind and thereby transform you.

I have a confession to make. I have about as much mechanical ability as a girl scout. When something goes wrong with my car I don't have the faintest idea what is going on. That used to bother me in my younger days. I would be out on a date and my car would break down. My male ego would not allow me to admit my ignorance, so I would get out and open up the hood, rattle my hand around inside the engine, slam the hood down, walk back to the car and hope it would start. Today, however, I make no pretense about my ignorance of mechanics. When something goes wrong with my car, I don't fool around with it. I take it to my mechanic and turn it over to him and allow him to overhaul it. Now that's precisely what we have in verses 1 and 2. You are not told to renew your mind. You are told to allow the indwelling Spirit of God to renew your mind. He's the renewer, not you (*see* Titus 3:5). He is willing to renew your mind, but you must make the presentation of your total self. As you do make yourself totally available to Him, He then begins to renew your mind gradually. The gradual renewing of your mind will in turn transform (metamorphize) you. In this way you will not be allowing the world to conform you. This, in essence, is the message of Romans 12:1, 2. Now keep in mind this is a gradual, developmental process. You can't expect to turn your whole self over to the Lord today and instantaneously have twenty years of faulty thinking processes overcome! It has taken you twenty years to get these faulty habits, and it is going to take time for the Holy Spirit to slowly renew your mind.

All that is stated in Romans 12:1,2 with regard to allowing the Spirit to gradually transform you is simply another way of saying "Walk in the Spirit . . ." (Galatians 5:16). To walk in (by means of) the Spirit is to allow the indwelling Holy Spirit to control you. This is the same way you allow the Spirit to renew your mind. The point I wish to bring out at this juncture is that learning to walk is a slow, awkward, painful process! How does a child learn to walk? Does it suddenly jump to its feet, hurdle the crib, and start running around the room? No! It gradually learns to walk over a period of many months. The baby takes a feeble step and falls flat on its face. At first there is more stumbling than walking. Ever so gradually it learns how to walk. It's awkward and painful.

Practically speaking, Christians *learn* to walk in the Spirit. It seems terribly awkward at first and is often painful. Perhaps you are thinking that you will never get the hang of it. Don't get discouraged. It will gradually become more natural. Suppose a little baby, after taking a severe fall for the three thousandth time, would just lie on the floor and squall, "I've tried three thousand times and keep falling. I'll just never learn to walk!" You would probably say to the child, "Get up, you big baby! Everybody else has learned to walk and you can learn to walk. Just hang in there!"

It is true that some children learn to walk more quickly and with greater ease than others. Likewise some Christians learn to walk by the Spirit more rapidly than others. Regardless of this fact, all can and should learn to walk by means of the Spirit. Keep relentlessly at it. It will eventually become more natural.

Now let me wrap up in a brief capsule statement the essence of what we have seen in Romans 12:1,2. Learn to live in moment-by-moment total faith commitment to the indwelling Spirit. I have formed the habit of reminding myself of this commitment each morning. I find that I am a living sacrifice and, therefore, have a tendency to jump off God's altar, so to speak. Even during the day if I find that I am off in self-will trying to run the show, I pause and simply say, "Lord, I am Yours and seem to have forgotten it. Take over." If a persistently selfish thought begins to nag you, don't fight it. Commit it! Right on the spot ask the Lord to take over your mental machinery. It does not need to be a big ceremony. You don't have to spread out the prayer rug and face Mecca. Simply make a brief faith committal. You will be surprised how desirous the Lord is to see us do this. Learning to live in constant submission to the indwelling Spirit will seem awkward at first, but so did learning to roller skate. Remember?

Now, we must not only live in faith committal, but we must also correct the input. The Bible admonishes us to "Think on these things," not just any old thing! Your mind is like a fantastic computer. In the computer industry they have a trade word, GIGO. The word means "garbage in, garbage out!" In other words, the industry realizes that what comes out of a computer is a direct reflection of what is fed into it. The same thing is true with your mind. If you are serious about mental health, you must control what is put in via the ear gate and the eye gate. Don't be naive. You can't be reading filthy books; you can't be going to filthy movies and watching filthy TV shows; you can't be filling your mind with that kind of corruption and still maintain good mental health. You must discipline yourself regarding the kind of music to which you listen. I am not a connoisseur of music. I know next to nothing about what constitutes good or bad music. I only know what I like and don't like, but that makes it neither good nor bad. However, I *do know* what the words of a song mean! Some of the current songs have filthy lyrics. At times the filth is in code language and at other times it is not. In any case, it is pure filth. You can't have that filthy material drummed into your ears hour after hour and have good mental health. I want it to be perfectly clear that I am not just referring to teen-age tunes either. Some of the lyrics in current country and western music are suggestive also. So *correct the input.*

A third suggestion for your personal mental-hygiene program would be to keep your mind active. This is certainly implied in the biblical command: "Think on these things." As noted above, the tense of the verb indicates continuous action; hence it could be translated, *"Continuously think* on these things" (*see* Philippians 4:8). You have probably heard the old adage, "Idle hands are the devil's workshop." I think it would be more accurate to say, "An idle mind is the devil's workshop." I don't know about you, but whenever I do not have anything to actively engage my mind, my thoughts tend to move toward self. I begin to think selfish thoughts. So it is important to keep your mind active. A few months ago, a man came to me privately and confessed having a real problem with evil, lustful thoughts. After some probing, I discovered that most of his trouble came when he did not have anything to actively engage his mind. Watch those times when you are driving home from work. It is so easy to let your mind slip into neutral and then in come the selfish thoughts. At times like this, make an effort to "think on these things." Perhaps you can sing softly to yourself about our wonderful Lord. Even better, reach over and turn off that news broadcast. Then begin to review the Scripture verses that you have memorized. If you have never memorized Scripture, start a systematic program. The blessed man pictured in Psalms 1 did not go around with his brains in limbo. Rather he constantly meditated on God's Word (see Psalms 1:2). Did not David, the man after God's heart, say, "Thy word have I hid in mine heart, that I might not sin against thee" (Psalms 119:11). You will find that good mental hygiene will be but one of many practical benefits of a regular program of Scripture memorization. Don't let your mind grow fat and sloppy. Don't let it become lazy. Keep it active.

By way of conclusion, (1) Realize the importance of mental health. I think that once you start to realize how important it is, it will be a big factor in beginning to really take the whole matter seriously. (2) Recognize that God holds you responsible for what you think. (3) Accept the fact that it is not going to be a one-shot deal. There is no one thing you can do to have instant mental health. It has taken you fifteen or twenty years to develop faulty thought patterns, and it may take time for the Holy Spirit to gradually renew your mind. (4) Guard what you allow to enter your mind via the eye or ear gate. (5) Keep your mind active. Watch those times when there is nothing to actively engage your mind. (6) Above all, learn to walk by means of the Holy Spirit. Learn to live in moment-by-moment faith committal, and (7) Remember that it will seem awkward at first. Keep in mind the analogy of roller skating. As you learn to live in moment-by-moment faith committal with ever increasing consistency, the Holy Spirit will be renewing your mind and thereby changing you. As this change takes place, and it most certainly will, the reality of Isaiah 26:3, "Thou wilt keep him in perfect peace, whose mind is stayed on thee . . ." will become a reality in your life. The more one's mental machinery is under control of the Lord, the greater will be his inward peace regardless of the external circumstances. Such a person will begin to experience that "good, and acceptable, and perfect, will of God" (Romans 12:2).

6

Playing on God's Team

I think if I had one special criticism to level against the average Christian it would not be that they are doing something so terribly wrong, but the fact that they are not really doing anything! They seem to be content to just occupy time and space in this world —a world that is falling apart around us! A world that desperately needs the message that we have! In such a situation an apathetic satisfaction with the status quo is tragic. To content oneself with simply being a nice guy is lamentable.

It reminds me of the story concerning an elderly spinster named Nancy Jones. Miss Jones lived in a small midwestern community. She had the notoriety of being the oldest resident of the town. One day she died and the editor of the local newspaper wanted to print a little caption commemorating Miss Jones's death. However, the more he thought about it, the more he became aware that while Miss Jones had never done anything terribly wrong (she had never spent a night in jail, or had ever been drunk), yet she had never actually done anything of note. While musing over this, the editor went down to have his morning coffee and met the owner of the tombstone establishment in the little community. He poured out his soul to him. The tombstone proprietor stated that he had been having the same problem. He wanted to put something on Miss Jones's tombstone besides, "Miss Nancy Jones, born such-and-such a date and died such-and-such a date," but he couldn't think of anything of significance that she had ever done. The editor decided to go back to his office and assign the first reporter he came across the task of writing up a small article suitable for both the paper and the tombstone. Upon returning to the office, the only fellow around was the sports editor, so he gave him the assignment. They tell me if you pass through that little community you will find the following statement on her tombstone:

Here lies the bones of Nancy Jones,
   for her life held no terrors.

She lived an old maid. She died an old maid.
   No hits, no runs, no errors.

Now I don't know about you, but I don't want that to be said of me. When I depart from this life, I want my life to have counted for something. I want to have made some sort of positive contribution for the glory of God.

Many Christians have such a misconception of Christian service. We seem to have the idea that Christian service is the Christian doing God a favor. You know the "I'm going to do something for Jesus" philosophy. Actually, in the thinking of many, the fellow who can get out of jobs in the church is the sharp guy. The brother who allows himself to be elected for various responsibilities in the church is the stupid idiot. This only shows us what a terrible misconception we have of serving the Lord. Christian service is not *you* doing something for *Jesus*. Christian service is having the high and holy privilege of having God take you as an instrument in His hand and of doing some significant things through you. That's Christian service.

A few years ago, Willie Mays, who at that time was with the San Francisco Giants, broke the home-run hitting record. I still remember the night up at Candlestick Park when Willie walked up to the bat rack. He was only one home run away from breaking the National League record. He fingered a few of the bats in the rack, and out of all of the two dozen bats he selected one instrument, and with that bat he stepped up to the plate and proceeded to break the National League home-run hitting record. I imagine if bats could talk, that one bat is still bragging about the fact that of all the bats in the rack, it alone was selected by Willie Mays to break the National League home-run hitting record. Now that's Christian service. That's being used of God. That's having the high and holy privilege of having God take you like an instrument and perform His mighty task through you.

There is no greater privilege that you and I will ever have than to be used of God. If we begin to get the proper perspective we would not consider ourselves as having been done a disservice to have been put on a church committee. The Sunday-school superintendent would not have to go around begging for teachers and other workers to keep the program going. If we really had our priorities in proper focus, there would be waiting lines to fill positions in the church and Sunday school.

Now the obvious fact is this. Most Christians, like Nancy Jones, are not being significantly used in the service of the King. They are simply occupying time and space on the planet. Why is this true? In reality only a few ever really know the excitement and thrill of having God effectively use their lives. Not only is this a fact of life, but it is a fact of Scripture. At the conclusion of a parable dealing with serving the Lord (Matthew 20:1-15), Christ said, " . . . many be called, but few chosen" (v. 16). In this context the statement must pertain to Christian service. It almost seems in the context of the parable that God invites all of His disciples (the many) to have the privilege of serving Him; but though the privilege is available to all (the many), only a very few actually realize that privilege. Out of the *many* that are invited, only a *few* are actually chosen. I don't know about you, but I want to be one of those chosen few. I want to be one of those few among the many whom

God chooses to use. It's like a football team at a large university. There may be a hundred men on the squad and all are eligible to be used in the game. The coach would like to use all of them, but when it comes time to play, only eleven out of the hundred are chosen. To be selected by the coach, to be used in the game is considered a privilege. A football player doesn't say, "Oh, please coach, choose someone else." No. It's a privilege and that is what Christian service is. It is the privilege of being chosen by God to be used for His glory!

But why is it that God isn't using more Christians? Is it because God is arbitrary? Does God play favorites? No! It's because God has standards. When the football coach starts selecting the eleven men out of a hundred, he is looking for certain qualities of excellence in those men. The men who match up to certain standards have the privilege of being used in the game, while the others sit on the bench. All are members of the football team, but only those few who meet standards of excellence are used in the game. Following this analogy, if you are a Christian you are on God's great team, but that doesn't mean you are going to have the privilege of being used unless you are able to meet certain standards. What are these standards?

I have found a verse in the New Testament that brings together in one simple statement the qualifications that God looks for in selecting men He will use to accomplish His purposes. I promise you that if you meet these standards, God will use your life in a significant manner. These qualifications are stated succinctly in 1 Peter 3:15: "But sanctify the Lord God in your hearts: and be ready always to give an answer to every man that asketh you a reason of the hope that is in you with meekness and fear." The writer seems to be saying that if certain conditions prevail in your life, you will be ready when God sends people your way and you will have the exciting experience of being used.

Now what are the qualities? The first is stated in the words, "But sanctify the Lord God in your hearts. . . ." The root meaning of the word *sanctify* is to "set apart" or to "separate." If you are ever going to be used of God, you must be a separated Christian. Perhaps you are saying, "Boy, am I ever separated. I don't go to dirty movies, I don't read *Playboy* magazine. I'm really a separated Christian." Yet separation *from* sin is only half the picture. To be sure it is necessary to be separated *from* evil, but are you separated *to* anything? There is both a negative and positive aspect to bibilical separation. Notice what Paul says in Romans 1:1: "Paul, a servant of Jesus Christ, called to be an apostle, separated unto the gospel of God." Paul was not only separated from sin, but he was separated in a positive way to the task of getting out the Good News of Jesus Christ. In other words, Paul was totally dedicated to God. It is this positive aspect of separation that we have in 1 Peter 3:15: ". . . sanctify the Lord God in your hearts." God must be number one in our lives or we'll never really have the privilege of having God use us in a significant manner. A lot of Christians try to hold on to God with one hand, and the world with the other. God will never use a person like that.

Some years ago I was a youth minister at a rather large church. We had a banquet for our teen-agers and invited a varsity football player to come and talk to the young people. At that time UCLA was the big powerhouse in Southern California football. They had an outstanding coach named Red Sanders. Our speaker was not only a member of this great team, but was an All-American. He came and talked to our young people and told them, "If anyone wants to play football for Coach Red Sanders, they have to be totally dedicated to football." He said that football would have to be their life, their food, their girl friend. He said if they weren't totally dedicated to football, they would never be able to play football for Red Sanders. This is precisely the type of dedication that's alluded to in the statement, "But sanctify the Lord God in your hearts. . . ." The primary requirement to being used of God is to be totally dedicated to Him. This is essentially the same thing that Paul tells us in Romans 12:1: "I beseech you therefore, breth-

ren, by the mercies of God, that ye present your bodies a living
sacrifice, holy, acceptable unto God, which is your reasonable
service." It's virtually the same thing that Christ said in Matthew
10:39: "He that findeth his life shall lose it: and he that loseth his
life for my sake shall find it." God's ways are so often the opposite
of ours. God says, "Throw your life away to Me and I'll use you."
Total dedication. Sanctify the Lord God in your heart.

Now notice the next phrase in our verse, "and be ready"
(1 Peter 3:15). This speaks of preparation. Herein lies a second
qualification for the man who would know the excitement of
being used of God. God wants not only dedication but preparation. I am persuaded that many of God's people are not selected
to be used as instruments in God's hand simply because they are
not ready. They are not prepared to do a job for God. Have you
sat in a church service and heard people recount exciting inci-
dents of how God used their lives and wish that God would use
you like that? Well, are you ready? Are you prepared to do a job?
I have a friend who is a butcher. He has a workbench in his shop
and above it are a bunch of knives: long knives, short knives, fat
knives, skinny knives. Let's imagine that there are two knives
above the workbench that are identical. They have the same
blade length, same shape, same handle, same quality of steel.
However, one knife is sharp and the other dull. Should my friend
decide to use one of the two knives in cutting up a side of beef,
which do you think he would select? Obviously he would use the
sharp knife! The instrument that is *ready* is the instrument that is
used.

In one of the churches I pastored, there were very few such
men. In fact, I only had one man that I considered a real, faithful
individual. One day as I was greeting the people after the service,
this man walked by and told me that he wanted me to come by
his house the following week to talk to a little neighbor boy who
wanted to know how to get to heaven. I thought, "God help us.
I thought I had one prepared man in this church and he doesn't

even know how to tell a little neighbor boy how to get to heaven." Would you know what to tell your neighbor? Maybe that is why God isn't using you. You are not ready. You're not prepared to do a job for Him. I'm personally persuaded that this is the major reason that keeps most Christians from being effectively used of God.

How does a person get ready? I can think of no better way than to follow the admonition of 2 Timothy 2:15: "Study to shew thyself approved unto God, a workman that needeth not to be ashamed, rightly dividing the word of truth." I would remind you that the first word in the verse is an imperative. That means it's a command. God commands you to study. Just as God commands you to preach the gospel to every creature, and to walk in love and be filled with the Spirit, He also commands you to study. If you are not studying God's Word consistently, you are disobeying the command of God. In both Greek and English dictionaries the word *study* means "to give diligence." It means more than sitting and listening to good sermons. It means more than sitting and enjoying good Bible lessons. You can do these things and never study. You can sit and enjoy a good lesson in your church and walk out the door and if you never study the lesson, do you know what will probably happen? You'll forget 90 percent of it. Perhaps that's why you know so little of the Bible even after attending a good church for years. That's probably why God is not using you effectively. You are not ready because you have not studied to meet God's approval as an unashamed workman!

I find that most Christian people have never been programmed to study God's Word and as a consequence are extremely ignorant of the teachings of the Bible. I had a friend some years ago who was called to take the pulpit in one of the largest churches on the West Coast. The pastor of that church was probably one of the greatest Bible teachers on the West Coast at that time. This man had been expounding the Scriptures at that church for thirty years. My friend was called to take his place. He naturally thought, "What can I possibly tell these people that they don't already know? They have had the very best Bible exposition for thirty years." My friend hit upon a plan. One Wendesday night he administered, without warning, a simple Bible examination in order to discover their level of biblical knowledge. He was amazed at their ignorance! They didn't know anything. Now what had happened? They had had the best by way of Bible instruction for thirty years, but they were ignorant because they had never *studied.* They had never given diligence. They had never obeyed God in this command. They were living mediocre, miserable Christian lives because they had never really studied. Could you pass such an examination? Are you missing the excitement of God using your life because you have been disobeying His command to study?

We find at Biola College that young people come programmed to study history, mathematics, and psychology, but not to study Bible. They have been programmed to sit and enjoy Bible lectures. It's quite a shock to those young people when I give my first five-week examination! All of a sudden they discover that they've got to study the Bible just like they do English or history and all of their other subjects. Some of you have attended your church for twenty years and yet have never studied the Bible. Then you wonder why your life isn't counting for Christ. I want to challenge you to begin to get ready by beginning to study. All things being equal, you will find that God will use you in proportion to the degree you prepare yourself by systematic study of His Word. Make an effort to get the truths of the Bible into your mind. It takes work. It takes labor. That's what studying is all about. There is no easy way.

There are numerous methods by which you can implement a program of study. Perhaps the most logical thing to do is to begin to avail yourself of the biblical instruction that you have in your local church each week. Do you realize that in your church you probably have four hours of biblical instruction every week? You

have a Sunday-school class. You have a morning and evening
service on Sunday. You have a midweek Bible study. Let me
challenge you to begin to bring a notebook to church and Sunday
school and take notes on the lessons and sermons you hear. Even
the process of taking notes will help you retain the information.
Then go home and reorganize those notes. All of this will be a
learning process. Then make a concentrated effort during the
week to assimilate as much of the information as you can. Perhaps
married couples can work together on this as a project. The four
hours of biblical material available in your church could well serve
as a basis for your study the entire week. With such a program of
study, educators tell us you will probably retain from 70 to 80
percent of the significant material. How could you possibly pass
a course in college if you just sat and enjoyed the lectures? I want
to challenge you to treat biblical instruction as you would a four-
unit class at a university. Do this for six months and I promise you
that you will be pleasantly surprised at the biblical knowledge you
are achieving, and best of all God will begin to use your life!

Perhaps you do not attend a church where solid biblical instruction is forthcoming. In that case, why not investigate the possibility
of receiving biblical instruction via the radio? In virtually every
area of this nation a person can tune in excellent Bible-centered
radio programs. I would urge that you consult some reliable Christian friend to determine a suitable program in your area. Another
idea would be Bible correspondence courses. This is an excellent
method, especially for those of us who need the added motivation
of deadlines, tests, et cetera. Check with your pastor or a Christian
friend and I am sure they can direct you to some excellent
courses. (Moody Bible Institute in Chicago has a number of excellent Bible correspondence courses.)

If you live in the area of a Bible institute, Christian college, or
seminary, why not investigate the possibility of taking one Bible
course a semester, either for audit or credit? Many schools have
evening Bible classes. I have a dentist friend auditing two of my

classes at Biola at the present time. He is determined to gain the necessary biblical knowledge to "be ready . . . to give an answer. . . ." He desires to meet the approval of God as a workman that needeth not to be ashamed.

Thus far we have seen that God is looking for dedicated and prepared workmen, but a careful look at our passage will reveal yet one more qualification. The passage reads, "But sanctify the Lord God in your hearts and be ready *always*. . . ." The admonition is not to be ready some of the time or whenever you feel in the mood, but always. This speaks of *fidelity*. The New Testament makes it very clear that God demands faithfulness of those who will play on His team. God will not use you in any significant manner unless you can demonstrate dependability. In the words of Jesus: "Be ye faithful in little things, and I will make you ruler over much," (*see* Matthew 25:23). Note the requirement is to prove fidelity in little things before the privilege of greater things. Paul insists that fidelity is a *requirement* for God's servants (*see* 1 Corinthians 4:2). It is not just nice, it is necessary! You don't have to be good-looking to be used of God. You really don't have to be talented to have God use you, but you do have to be faithful. God will not use you unless you show Him that you are dependable in little things. God doesn't want racehorses, he wants plow horses. When a racehorse breaks out of the gate he's really going, but he only runs for a few minutes and then he has had it. God wants plow horses. An old plow horse may move slowly, but he moves consistently. Can God depend on you for little things like faithful church attendance? If not, then don't expect to be used in greater things. If you are given a position as the third member of the popcorn committee do it faithfully as unto the Lord. If your job is straightening up the chairs after the meeting is over, can God count on you for that? Until God can count on you for little things, He won't use you.

I was called to be a pastor of a little church after being in seminary one year. In that church I had a man who had an excellent knowledge of the Bible. He actually knew more about the Bible than I did, but I couldn't even use that man to teach a Sunday school class. Do you know why? He was unfaithful. I know of seminary graduates who are on the sidelines today because of their lack in this area.

God desires to use every believer, but He has standards. There are qualifications. That is true in most activities. The state of California has standards. Not just anyone can cut hair in the state. Not just anyone can teach school. Not just anyone can be a beautician. Individuals must measure up to certain standards of excellence. So it is with God, and to the degree that you measure up to these three qualifications of dedication, preparation, and dependability you will be used of God. He will take you like an instrument in His mighty hand and accomplish His purposes through you. You will know the thrill of being one of the chosen few. Your life will take on a new glow and excitement. To be sure we are each different, so God will not use all in the same way, but each can and should be used in accordance with his own individual personality. Then one of these days when you stand before your Lord you will be able to say with Paul, "I have fought a good fight, I have finished my course, I have kept the faith. Henceforth there is laid up for me a crown of righteousness, which the Lord, the righteous judge, shall give me at that day" (2 Timothy 4:7,8).

7

Faith Turns It All On

No book on Christian living could possibly be considered complete without a discussion of *faith.*

Faith is absolutely basic to successful Christ-centered living. How did you become a Christian? By faith. How are you to live your daily Christian life? By faith. In fact, the total duty of the Christian can be summed up in one word—*belief.* One day, certain men came to Christ and asked, "How can we work the works of God?" Christ replied, "This is the work of God, that ye believe . . ." (John 6:29).

Every blessing of God must be appropriated by faith. Moody likened faith to a hand that reaches out to take the blessings of God. Christians are loaded with all kinds of spiritual goodies (*see* Ephesians 1:3), but all too often they live like paupers because they either don't understand what they have, or don't know how to utilize what they have. We are like a big 747 jet loaded with potential, but until somebody turns on the key, that potential is of no value. Faith is that key.

A great many of our problems in practical Christian living can be traced back to a basic lack of faith. For example, consider the problem of worry. Every time you and I worry about something what are we really saying? We are actually saying, "God, I don't think you can hack this one!" Let's face it, this is a lack of faith! For another example, take a good look at the problem of a poor self-image. How can any Christian possibly have a poor self-image? When a Christian suffers from a poor self-image, it is usually because he does not really believe who he is in Christ Jesus. Let any Christian really believe who he is in Christ and he can't possibly suffer from an image deficiency. Finally, consider the problem of loneliness. Why is a Christian lonely? No Christian is *ever* alone! Did not our Lord say, "I am with you alway"? (Matthew 28:20). He has promised that He will never leave you or forsake you. Christian, when you are lonely you do not really believe these promises of our Lord. Likewise, when a Christian feels guilty it can often be traced to a lack of confidence in the total forgiveness of God *(see* Romans 8:33, 34). Lack of faith is ultimately behind all disobedience. If I truly believed God and His Word, I would never deliberately violate it. When I do, I'm actually saying, "Lord, I don't really believe you." The words of the old song "Trust and Obey" are theologically correct. If you really trust, you will obey. So faith is crucial to many areas of Christian living.

What is faith? How does faith grow and develop? Until you learn how to have an aggressive growing faith, you can't effectively appropriate the blessings and provisions of God.

First of all, *what is faith?* The closest thing we have in the Bible to a formal definition of faith is found in Hebrews 11:1. Some would argue that even this verse is not actually a definition. Yet all would agree that it is as close as the Bible ever comes to a definition. I consider it a very fine definition of the subject. The passage reads: "Now faith is the substance of things hoped for, the evidence of things not seen." First let's make a brief study of the actual word *faith.* The word *faith* means *trust.* It means *firm persuasion.* It is used 243 times in various forms in the New Testament, thus it is a very important biblical word. The word involves three things: knowledge, acceptance, and appropriation. Let's thus consider knowledge as intellectual awareness. In order to exercise faith you must have knowledge. You must know certain facts. For example, in order for me to exercise faith in a chair

I've got to know that the chair exists, and pertinent facts about the chair (i.e. size, strength, et cetera). Next, I must accept those facts as true. I must accept the fact that the chair is there, that the chair is made of a sturdy metal, that it is capable of holding my weight. This we call acceptance: knowledge first, then acceptance.

But, you can have both knowledge and acceptance and yet fail to exercise true biblical faith. Some people have taken these first two steps, but have never taken the third and crucial step. Some would call this two-step type of faith "believing only with the head." By way of example, I can stand and look at a chair. I can know of the chair's existence and can accept the facts that my senses convey to me about that chair, yet the chair itself would be doing nothing for me. What must I do in order for that chair to be of practical benefit to me? I must sit on it. Now what am I doing when I sit on it? I am appropriating the things that I know and have accepted to be true. I am trusting in it. I am depending on it. You haven't really exercised biblical faith until you take this third step of *appropriation.* A lot of people only exercise a two-step faith in Jesus Christ.

I dare say a good percentage of the people in your community know about Jesus Christ. They've heard how He died on the cross, was buried, and rose again. Most of these people would accept these facts as true, yet they have never been regenerated. For years I had taken these first two steps without ever being saved. I believed that Jesus was a real person. I believed that He existed in history. I accepted these historical facts as true, yet I was a lost sinner all of that time because I had never taken the third crucial step. I was exercising the same kind of faith that I exercise with regard to Columbus. I believe that Columbus discovered some off-shore islands in 1492. I accept those facts as true, but I am not exercising real faith in Columbus. I am not trusting him to do anything for me. I simply have an intellectual knowledge and acceptance of the facts of history about him. Biblical faith is taking that third step of appropriation.

Let me pursue biblical faith one step further. Biblical faith involves submission. Take the chair, for example. When I appropriate the chair, when I sit down on it and depend on it, am I not in that very process submitting myself to the chair? When you sit on a chair you are in submission to it. So biblical faith involves submission. You cannot have real faith in Christ without submitting to Him. Using the analogy of a lifeguard, if you depend on the lifeguard to save you, you must at the same time submit to him.

Let us now move beyond consideration of the bare word *faith* to the formal statement of Hebrews 11:1. Notice the wording, "Now faith is the substance of things hoped for, the evidence of things not seen." Let's consider some characteristics of biblical faith based upon this statement. Biblical faith is based on evidence. The evidence of things not seen. Biblical faith is not blind. Biblical faith looks at *all* of the facts, considers *all* of the evidence and thereby comes to full conviction. Notice I underline the word *all*. Biblical faith considers not only the evidence that can be seen, but also the evidence that cannot be seen. Biblical faith then is not a leap in the dark. It is conviction based on all the evidence. Not all definitions listed in current dictionaries will fit biblical faith. One dictionary defines faith as "belief which is not based on truth." That particular definition is certainly not descriptive of biblical faith. Another dictionary states simply that faith is "belief without evidence." This is not biblical faith either. Faith is based on evidence and it is based on *all* of the evidence.

Perhaps the greatest Old Testament example of faith is to be found in the example of Abraham. How did Abraham's faith function? In Romans 4:17-21 we are given marvelous insight into the *modus operandi* of Abraham's faith. Notice the exact statement, "(As it is written, I have made thee a father of many nations,) before him whom he believed, even God, who quickeneth the dead, and calleth those things which be not as though they were. Who against hope believed in hope, that he might become the father of many nations, according to that which was spoken,

So shall thy seed be. And being not weak in faith, he considered not his own body now dead, when he was about an hundred years old, neither yet the deadness of Sarah's womb: He staggered not at the promise of God through unbelief; but was strong in faith, giving glory to God; And being fully persuaded that, what he had promised, he was able to perform." Now, unfortunately, the King James translation can be misleading when it says, "He considered not his own body now dead . . . [he considered not] the deadness of Sarah's womb." A person might get the idea that Abraham refused to consider the evidence. This was not the case at all. The statement literally reads, "He considered his body now dead. . . . He considered the deadness of Sarah's womb." Abraham looked at all of the evidence. He looked it full in the face. Biblical faith is not sticking your head in the sand and not paying attention to the facts. But let's get back to Abraham. God had promised him that he was going to have a son. Abraham got old. He looked at his body and said, "Old boy, you've had it! It is biologically impossible for you to father a child." Then he looked at his wife and said, "Old girl, you've had it also. It is biologically impossible for you to be a mother!" He fully considered all visible evidence. However, the facts you can see are not *all* of the facts. He also looked at the evidence of things not seen. He looked at the promise of God and having considered *all* the facts seen and unseen, he chose to believe God. He was fully persuaded that what God had promised He was able to perform! That is biblical faith.

Another example of a man considering unseen evidence may be found in the life of Noah. Notice what Scripture says about him. "By faith Noah, being warned of God of things not seen as yet . . ." (Hebrews 11:7). Noah had perhaps never even seen a raindrop and certainly he had never seen a holocaust anything like the flood, yet God warned him about it. That was evidence and Noah believed that evidence he could not see. How do we know he believed it? He built the ark. That is how we know he believed it. There was no reason for him to build the ark if he did not believe the evidence of things not seen. His obedience demonstrates his faith.

So faith looks at all of the evidence. Biblical faith is based upon evidence and the surest evidence in all the world is something you can't see with your physical eye—the categorical promises of God. The promises of God are the best possible evidence, but you can't see them, you can't put them in a test tube; and for this reason, some men reject them as evidence. I have never seen the present ministry of Christ, but I believe it and I have evidence for it. I have the promise of God. What better evidence could I possibly want?

Not only is faith based upon evidence, but it begets hope. Notice he says, "Now faith is the substance of things hoped for. . . ." "Substance of things hoped for," can be translated, "assurance of things hoped for." Biblical hope is different from human hope. When we use *hope* in ordinary speech it means 'desire.' For instance, a student might say, "I hope to make an *A* in my history class." There is a great deal of doubt in such a statement. He is desirous of making an *A* in the class, but he doesn't have the assurance that he is going to get it. In biblical hope there is *never* a question as to whether or not you will get the thing hoped for. Biblical hope means that you are absolutely sure you will get it. The only question you are uncertain about is *when* you will get it. That's biblical hope. Real faith begets this kind of hope. You anticipate getting things that you do not have right now and you *know* that you are going to get them, but the only question is you don't know exactly when you're going to get them.

May I say that you can't have real legitimate hope without faith. Faith and hope go together. Faith results in hope. If there is not faith, there can be no hope. Today we are living in a society which has lost virtually all faith. Men today do not have any faith in their government, in their fellowman, or in their God. They don't have much faith in their money. Seemingly they have little faith in anything! As a result, you don't see much hope around, do you? Without faith one cannot have hope. What is the current philosophy of the day? It's existentialism, commonly known as the *philosophy of despair*. The existentialist says, "There is not going to be a tomorrow. We're going to choke to death on smog. We're going to blow this planet apart. You might just as well not plan for tomorrow because there probably won't be a tomorrow." So what do they recommend? They say, "Just live for today. Just reach out in desperation and try and get some meaning in the moment. Get it with sex or pot, but get it and get it now." That is why the current generation is often called the Now Generation.

A beautiful illustration of the correlation between faith and hope was recently brought to my attention. The head of our science department at Biola College was asked to go to a local science teachers' association and give a presentation of creationism. Recently a law was passed making it mandatory for all science teachers in public high schools in the state to present both the theory of evolution and the theory of creation. These science teachers were now required by law to teach something of which they knew nothing, so they asked Dr. Kurtz to come down and present the creationists' point of view. They didn't ask him to come down and debate, they just asked him to present the viewpoint. In order to talk about creation, however, one must talk about God and that struck a nerve. The result was that the science teachers challenged Dr. Kurtz's stand. Of course Dr. Kurtz is well qualified to defend his position, having spent eight years on the faculty at UCLA before coming to Biola. They said, "Why do you teach creation and not evolution?" He began to give reasons why we taught creation rather than evolution. One of the reasons was stated as follows, "For years I had taught evolution at UCLA and I had no hope. Now that I am teaching creation I have hope." One science teacher said, "Sir, I resent that. I teach evolution and I want you to know that I have hope." Dr. Kurtz replied, "Lady, what is your hope?" She said, "My hope is to be recycled!" Well? I suppose you could vaguely describe that as hope, but what a miserable hope. Yet what else do they have? Without faith there is no legitimate hope. So faith is solid confidence based on evidence that begets a genuine hope.

Now, let's move to a consideration of another matter that is crucial in our study of faith—the *object* of faith. Actually, faith is of no more value than its object. A person can have a great deal of faith in a sinking ship, but it is of no value. You and the ship will go under anyway. Confidence in that ship is of no value if it's not a worthy ship, so the object of faith is of tremendous importance. Faith in an improper, inadequate object is of no value.

We might also point out that faith *demands* an object. The word *believe* is a transitive verb. You must believe in something. My theological skin crawls every time I hear a certain song that goes something like this, "Every time I hear a newborn baby cry, I believe." Well, what do you believe? In what do you believe? You must believe in something! You must have faith in someone! At times people will say, "Have faith." However, they have no concept of any object for that faith. This is not biblical faith. Biblical faith must have an object. It is important to clearly understand the object of biblical faith. The writer of the Book of Hebrews realized this, because after defining biblical faith (11:1) and revealing a few of the fantastic things that this kind of faith can accomplish (vs. 2-5), he proceeds to discuss the object of faith. He says, " . . . without faith it is impossible to please him: for he that cometh to God must believe that he is, and that he is a rewarder of them that diligently seek him." (v. 6). Notice it's something you must do. They that come to God in faith must do two things. It is a necessity. You must believe that God is and that He is the rewarder of them that diligently seek Him. Actually in these two statements which are really two aspects of the same thing, you have the two aspects of the object of biblical faith. I choose to call one the *ultimate object* of biblical faith and the other the *immediate object* of biblical faith.

The writer first discusses the ultimate object. They that come to God must believe that "He is." The expression *God is* comes from the verb "to be." You must believe that God *exists.* In the Bible, faith always ultimately rests in a person. In biblical faith the ultimate repose will always be in the *person of God.* Not everyone realizes this. Some people think you must have faith in the promises of God, or faith in your requests to God. However, these are not the ultimate objects of faith. It is always in the person of God. Faith goes beyond what you are asking God to do to confidence in the God who is going to do it. By way of example, consider Mark 11:22-26. Christ is seen giving one of His great statements about faith as it pertains to prayer. Notice His statement in verses 23 and 24: "For verily I say unto you, That whosoever shall say unto this mountain, Be thou removed, and be thou cast into the sea; and shall not doubt in his heart, but shall believe that those things which He saith shall come to pass; he shall have whatsoever he saith. Therefore I say unto you, What things soever ye desire, when ye pray, believe that ye receive them, and ye shall have them." Now if you read only these verses you might well say, "The ultimate object of faith is to believe in the things for which you ask." Notice, however, how the Lord begins the whole discussion: "And Jesus answering saith unto them, Have faith in God" (v. 22). The ultimate object of your faith is not to be the thing for which you are asking, not faith in your requests. It is not even to be faith in your faith! Rather it is to be *faith in God.* Actually, if you really analyze the entire matter logically, it is impossible to trust God's promises without ultimately trusting in the God who is making the promises. For instance, if I said to you, "If you will meet me at 3:00 P.M., I promise I will give you a hundred dollars." It would really be impossible for you to believe my promise without ultimately having confidence in me as a person. So the ultimate object in biblical faith is always resting in the person of God—God's *total* person. This means you are resting your confidence in God's *power,* in God's *wisdom,* in God's *love.*

Now, having set forth the ultimate object of faith, the writer then begins to talk about what we might call the *immediate* object of faith. He proceeds by saying: "They that come to God must believe that He is and that He is a rewarder of them that diligently seek Him." The immediate object of faith then is that "God is a rewarder of them that diligently seek Him." In other words, you must believe certain *facts* about God. Within the statement, "God is a rewarder of them that diligently seek Him," is the implication that God can *act.* Implied in that statement is the concept that God can act *intelligently.* Implied in that statement is the fact that God can and does act *morally.* So the immediate object of faith is the *facts* that God has revealed about Himself. Believing these facts leads us to ultimately believe in the person who revealed the facts. Faith rests immediately upon the knowledge that God has graciously given concerning Himself. Notice the example of faith in the life of Abraham found in Genesis, chapter fifteen. God had been making Abraham fantastic promises. God assured Abraham that he was to have a son. Abraham began to ask God to be more specific. Notice verses 3-6, "And Abram said, Behold, to me thou hast given no seed: and, lo, one born in my house is mine heir." God responded to Abraham's complaint. " . . . behold, the word of the Lord came unto him, saying, This shall not be thine heir; but he that shall come forth out of thine own bowels shall be thine heir. And he brought him forth abroad, and said, Look now toward heaven, and tell the stars, if thou be able to number them: and he said unto him, So shall thy seed be. And he believed in the Lord; and he counted it to him for righteousness." Now what is involved in Abraham believing *in the Lord?* It means that Abraham believed certain facts that God had given him about what He was going to do and what He promised. Yet, by believing those facts that God had given him, Abraham believed in the Lord. The immediate object of Abraham's faith was the facts that God had revealed to him, but this led to ultimate confidence in the God who revealed those facts. The immediate object of biblical faith is the factual statements that God gives us and this ultimately causes us to rest our confidence in the God who is giving us the information. Thus faith depends on doctrine. Faith depends on a Word from the Lord. Faith depends on God giving us certain factual statements about Himself. He factually tells us what He is going to do and how He operates. As we believe those facts immediately we ultimately believe in the person of God who is giving those facts.

This distinguishes faith from presumption. A great deal of what we call biblical faith is not faith at all but simply presumption. In order to exercise biblical faith you have to have facts from God. You must have a Word from God on the matter. Otherwise you have no basis for biblical faith. For instance, you might rush out on the freeway, begin to play mumblety-peg and say, "I'm going to trust God to take care of me." That would not be exercising biblical faith and they would probably scoop you up in a basket and haul you off to the morgue. In such a case you would not have any facts from God upon which to base your confidence. There- fore, you would be exercising presumption rather than faith. To exercise faith you must have a Word from God. Faith is founded upon the Word of God. If you don't have a Word from God on the matter, then you are not in a position to exercise faith. Now if God should tell you to go out on the freeway and play mumblety-peg and assure you that He would protect you, then you would have a factual basis for confidence. You would have a Word from the Lord on the matter and you would be perfectly safe. Without a Word from God, however, you are not exercising faith, you are exercising presumption. When I was a pastor, one of my members contracted terminal cancer. It was extremely painful. Day after day as I visited her she would look up at me and cry out, "Why?" Now I would love to have been able to tell her, "My sister, you are going to be healed tomorrow morning at precisely 8:00 A.M." But if I had made such a statement, it would not have been a statement of faith. It would have been a statement of presumption. I had no Word from God that she was going to be healed at 8:00 A.M. I could tell her, however, "My sister, God knows what is happening to you. God is concerned about what is happening to you and He desires nothing but the best for you. One of these days when you are in the glory, God is going to sit you down upon His knee, so to speak, and dry the tears from your eyes. At that time He will show you all of the reasons why He has allowed all of these things to happen to you. He will reveal all the reasons for every pain which has coursed through your body. At that moment you are going to say, 'Father, You've done the right thing. I wouldn't have had it any other way.' " Now I could tell her that in faith because I had a Word from God on that matter! Romans 8:28 states that, " . . . we know that all things work together for good to them that love God, to them who are the called according to his purpose."

Faith then is founded on knowledge. Biblical faith is not antagonistic to knowledge. Here is where many current ideas concerning faith differ from biblical faith. In the eyes of some people, faith is inferior to knowledge. Faith is not antagonistic to knowledge. Faith is not inferior to knowledge. Faith is *founded* on knowledge. Faith is not turning your mind into neutral. Faith is not sitting out on a rock, looking up into the sky, allowing your mind to go blank. Biblical faith is founded on knowledge. In order to exercise biblical faith you must know what God has promised. Only then can you put your confidence in those promises. Faith and knowledge go hand in hand. The more you know about the Bible, the more you know what God has promised, the more you will be able to exercise biblical faith.

Perhaps someone is saying, "If that is the case why does Christ commend childlike faith?" Let me assure you that it is not the *ignorance* of little children that Jesus commends. It is the child's sense of helplessness that Christ commends. It is the childlike willingness to receive of God that Christ commends.

So biblical faith is not just a nebulous communion with God, independent of the intellect, but biblical faith is founded upon the facts that God has given concerning Himself which causes us to ultimately have confidence in the God who is giving these facts. With that information, let's give a more expanded definition of faith. Faith is solid confidence in God based immediately upon the evidence of His Word and ultimately on His person; all of which produces genuine hope.

Next we want to consider *how faith grows.* Can faith develop? Is it possible for faith to grow? Let me say at the outset that biblical faith can and should grow. Just like a muscle can and should develop and grow stronger, so biblical faith should grow. You should have more confidence in God and His promises today than you had five years ago, and five years from now you should have more confidence in God and His Word than you do today.

Probably in modern times George Müller would be considered the greatest example of a man who could trust God for fantastic things. He ran an orphanage and would have fifty or so little children under his care. It would come time to feed them and he would not have any food in the house. Brother Müller would have the staff set the table and seat the children at the table. He would ask the blessing for the food they didn't have. What would happen? A milk wagon would break down outside, and the owner would give George Müller all of the milk! It is exciting to read his life story. Some people have said that Müller had a special gift of faith. Yet in his own autobiography, he denied any special gift of faith. Rather, he insisted that he had exactly the same faith that is resident in every believer. He insisted that his faith had grown ever so slowly over a period of sixty-nine years. As his faith grew, it became easier and easier to trust God for greater and greater things, until he could trust God for a thousand pounds as easily as it had previously been to trust Him for a few pence.

If you study the life of Abraham, you will find this is what happened to Abraham's faith. At first Abraham couldn't even trust God to leave home. He couldn't even trust God when his belly began to growl during a famine in Palestine. Because he didn't trust God to take care of him, he fled to Egypt and lied about his wife. Yet as you study the life of Abraham over a period of years, you will observe a gradual growth in his faith. His confidence in God slowly grew until he reached such a level of faith that God could tell him to kill his own son! Abraham didn't question God because he had learned to fully trust Him. Abraham didn't instantly become a great man of faith. His faith developed over a period of fifty years.

How does faith grow? It is crucial for us to learn this. Only then can we really appropriate the things that God has for us. In order for us to really understand how faith grows, we must consider some basic concepts with respect to faith. One crucial concept is that faith is subjective. Faith is engineered within a person, but though faith is subjective, it is stimulated by its object. In the case of faith in a political figure, it is the politician himself who stimulates faith within us. As we see what the politician does and how he acts and what he says, it stimulates confidence within us. The same process would be true of a philosophy or a religion. Confidence is inspired within us by the object. The object inspires the faith.

It is something in the object, be it a person or a philosophy, that stimulates faith within us; but what quality stimulates faith? What is it about the object that inspires confidence? What is it in a politician that causes people to develop confidence in him? What quality in a philosophy or a religion engenders almost fanatical faith in its followers? I submit that it is the quality of *truth*. As people see what they consider to be truth it inspires confidence. I don't think anybody ever consciously puts their confidence in a lie. In the case of the politician, people think they see the quality of truth in his dealings and that inspires confidence. As we see that the person is genuine, as we see that he is true blue, as we see that he is reliable, our faith is triggered. When people put their faith in charlatans, it is because they are deceived into thinking that the crook is true and genuine. They pull the wool over people's eyes. The people honestly think that these fellows are straight shooters. They don't consciously think that they are crooked. Nobody consciously puts his confidence in a falsehood.

If faith is stimulated by its object, then how do you get more faith? The more you know about the object, the more your faith will grow. This, of course, assumes that the object is true and genuine. If it is, then increasing knowledge of the object will mean a growing faith. Let's assume that a certain politician is a true person and I have a limited degree of confidence in him. How can my confidence in him grow? The more I get to know about him, the more I understand how he operates and what he is like, the more my faith will grow. We see this principle in Psalms 9:10, "And they that know thy name. . . ." *Name* in the Old Testament conveys the idea of character. To know the name of a person means to know the person. "They that know thy name will put their trust in thee." Knowing the object stimulates growth of faith in that object.

Now let's apply all of this to biblical faith. What is the object of biblical faith? Ultimately the object is God and immediately it is the facts we know about God. How do you get to know more about God? One way is by reading and contemplating the written revelation that God has given us concerning Himself. In the Bible we find out what God is like. We find out how He operates. We find out what He does and what He has done. All such knowledge will stimulate greater confidence in God. This is why Romans 10:17 says, "So then faith cometh by hearing, and hearing by the word of God." (This statement, in context, refers to saving faith, but saving faith is no different in quality than any other type of faith.) How does faith come? By hearing the Word of God. Why? Because as you really hear the Word of God, you get to know God that much better. You become aware of how He operates and what He has promised. All such knowledge stimulates faith within you. So the *Word of God* is *necessary* for growing faith! That is why I get disturbed by certain people within the Christian family who repudiate doctrine. They seem to want little to do with the Bible. All·they want to do is sit around and have an experience. This is not conducive to a growing faith. You can't separate a vigorous faith from a knowledge of this Book! You must hear what God is telling you. That is how faith comes. I am afraid that many young people have developed faith in a Christ that has been conjured up in their own minds. They have developed a faith in a Christ that is depicted in contemporary ballads, but it is not a confidence in the Christ of the Bible because they are not getting into the Bible to see what Christ is really like! This is crucial to a growing faith.

Now notice, "Faith cometh by hearing. . . ." It is possible to read the Bible and never hear what God is telling you. It is possible to even memorize Scripture and never hear what God is telling you. It is possible to study the Bible academically and never hear the Word. You can know all about the Antichrist's mother-in-law and never really hear what God is telling you. All of these mentioned above: reading the Bible, studying the Bible, memorizing the Bible, and so forth, can be *means* by which you can hear the Word, but just because you go through this ritual doesn't mean you *are* hearing what God is telling you. Hearing the Word means that you are really forcing yourself to face the implications of what God is telling you.

Let me share with you a method that I personally have discovered that forces me to hear the Word of God. Take, for example, a time when I am really worrying about something. As indicated at the beginning of this chapter, this is nothing more than lack of faith. It is caused by a basic lack of confidence in God. I care not how severe the problem, if the Lord is really my shepherd then I need not worry. With this powerful God, this loving God who is looking out for me, there is no reason under heaven to ever worry about anything. I need faith at that moment in order to stop worrying. I need my faith stimulated. How do I get faith? "Faith cometh by hearing, and hearing by the word of God." I need at that moment to really hear the Word of God so that my faith can be stimulated and I can really trust God. So I've developed a series of questions that I ask myself at such times. They force me to hear what God is telling me and thereby stimulate my faith so that I can really let God have the problem and, therefore, stop worrying about it. Now get the picture. I'm pacing the floor, the acid is dripping in my stomach, I can't sleep, so I say, "Now Mitchell, if you stay up all night and worry about this thing can you really do anything about it?" I force myself to face my own inadequacy because God's strength is made perfect in weakness. Then I ask the second question, "Mitchell, is God *able* to do anything about this problem?" Then I begin to read verses from the Bible concerning God's ability. They may be verses I have read a hundred times before, but at that moment I need to hear the Word of God. I will read of God's ability to create the heavens and earth, or how He fed 5,000 people at once. Pretty soon I am thoroughly convinced that God is more than adequate to handle my problem. In fact, I begin to realize that my problem is about the size of a peanut compared to His ability. Then I ask myself a third question, "Mitchell, is God *willing* to take your problem?" Then I look into the many promises of God. There are hundreds of them. I've read them all before, but at that moment I need to force myself to hear what God is telling me and to face the implications as to what He is saying—for instance, Philippians 4:19, ". . . my God shall supply all your need according to his riches in glory by Christ Jesus," or 1 Peter 5:7, "Casting all your care upon him; for he careth for you." Pretty soon I am thoroughly convinced that God is not only willing to take care of my problem, but that He is practically begging me to give it to Him. At that point I say, "Now look, Mitchell, you idiot. If you can't do anything about it anyway, and if God is more than adequate to handle it, and God is practically begging you to give it to Him, why don't you let Him have it and go to sleep?" I find that at this point my faith has been sufficiently stimulated to enable me to really let God have the problem. Of course, every time I do, the words of Philippians 4:7 are true experientially in my life, "And the peace of God, which passeth all understanding, shall keep your hearts and minds through Christ Jesus."

By this simple process I forced myself to hear God's Word and that stimulated my faith so that I could trust the Lord for the problem. So knowledge of the object stimulates faith. One of the finest ways of getting to know God is through His Word. By constantly hearing God's Word, by daily hearing what God is telling us in the Bible, we gradually find our faith stimulated. Our faith will gradually grow. It will not be instantaneous growth. Like physical growth, it is gradual. As you constantly eat meals you gradually grow. As you continually feed on God's Word, really hearing what God is telling you, your faith and confidence gradually grow. It is very much like getting to know a friend. All of us have a real close friend, a person in whom we have implicit confidence. How was such a faith relationship developed? Look back and reflect. Analyze the matter and you will discover that it didn't happen all at once. Such a relationship gradually evolved over years of personal interaction and observation. You saw your friend in times of danger react with bravery. You had seen your friend in times of perplexity respond with wisdom. You experienced sympathy from your friend when you came to him in times of trouble. Over a period of years of such observation, your faith in your friend grew slowly, yet grow it did, until you reached the point where now just a look or word from your friend causes you to respond with implicit trust. Thus, your faith has developed over the years as you became better and better acquainted with him.

This kind of relationship should be developing between you and the Lord. As you walk with Him and as you personally see that

He fulfills His promises, you will find yourself able to trust Him with ever increasing consistency. This is *walking by faith*—learning to trust Him more and more with every detail of your life. Then you will begin to realize in actual experience all of the spiritual blessings and potentialities that you have in Christ Jesus. You will be able to possess your possessions. Christ said, " . . . all things are possible to him that believeth" (Mark 9:23). Jesus seemed to attribute a sort of omnipotence to faith. It is not ultimately a question of what we can do or even what we can ask for in prayer, but *what we can believe!* Faith turns it all on!

8

Prayer Is Where the Action Is

My earliest recollection of life in the U.S. Navy is that first morning in boot camp. They rolled us out at daybreak, lined us up, and the drill instructor snarled, "Now men, you have your way of doing things and I have my way of doing things, but around here we are going to do things the navy way!" I wonder if this does not apply to the Lord's work. Often you have your ideas as to how God's work ought to be accomplished and I have my ideas, but I'm beginning to believe that there is another way that is different from your way and my way, and that's *God's way!*

Have you ever reflected upon the fact that God usually does not do things the way we do them? Would you have captured the city of Jericho by having your men walk around it and blow horns? Surely a very unusual way to conquer a city, but it worked because it was God's way! The fact is that we are categorically told that God's ways are not our ways (*see* Isaiah 55:8,9). One of the great problems in living our everyday Christian lives is that we insist upon doing things our way instead of God's way. We do not need *new* methods, we need desperately to get back to the *old* methods—the biblical methods.

Shortly before He went to the cross, Jesus gathered His eleven key men around Him for a final briefing session. These eleven men would be responsible (humanly speaking) for carrying out Christ's program on this earth after His Ascension. In this final crucial meeting (recorded in John 14-17), Jesus reiterated six times, "If you ask . . . I will do" (*see* John 14:13). Now, when Jesus Christ repeats something to His disciples six times in one meeting, you and I had better sit up and take notice. I submit to you that Jesus was giving His disciples a formula for action. He was telling them how to really accomplish things in divine style.

In this simple statement, prayer is envisioned as the *primary human factor in the accomplishment of the divine program on this earth.* With a startling boldness, Christ asserted that divine action, in some mysterious manner, is conditioned upon believing prayer. Prayer is thus set forth as the chief task of the believer. It is his responsibility to ask. It is God's responsibility to accomplish. James voiced much the same truth when he said, ". . . ye have not, because ye ask not" (4:2). The responsibility for asking is ours; the responsibility for doing is God's. When the believer does not ask, God is not responsible to *do,* and so the believer *has not.*

This twofold division of responsibility (i.e., our asking and God's doing) can be seen effectively at work in the early church. A close study of the Book of Acts will reveal that the believers fervently and persistently asked and God consistently accomplished. To be sure, God worked through human instrumentality, but close scrutiny reveals that it was divine (not human) power at work accomplishing mighty deeds.

In light of this, it is difficult to envision the successful functioning of God's program, be it individual or corporate, apart from the consistent and proper practice of prayer. In fact, it seems almost axiomatic that a failure in prayer will mean a failure in the effective functioning of the individual (or the group) so far as God's work is concerned.

Therefore it becomes self-evident that instruction relative to proper prayer practice is of the utmost importance to the disciple. The believer must not only ask, but he must also be careful not to ask *amiss,* or in the wrong way (*see* James 4:3). Our Lord's disciples evidently realized this fact. The one and only time they ever asked the Lord to teach them anything, it was for prayer instruction. In Luke 11:1 they urged, "Lord, teach us to pray." Evidently these men had noted that with Jesus, prayer was a force rather than a form. Indeed, they seemed to see prayer as the secret of spiritual success in the One whom they so much admired.

This request prompted the longest and most significant single instruction on prayer found anywhere in the Word of God (Luke 11:1-13). Perhaps no lesson is more desperately needed today among believers than this practical lesson on the *modus operandi* of prayer.

The most startling fact about this lesson is in what the Lord left *unsaid.* The Lord doesn't give His disciples trite little prayers to be recited in rote fashion. (Close study of the so-called Lord's Prayer reveals that it was never intended to be recited in a ritual manner.) The Lord said nothing about assuming a pious tone of voice when praying or using a particular stilted "prayer vocabulary." Many people revert unwittingly to the use of King James medieval English when they pray. Certainly, according to contemporary prayer practices, one would have expected instruction along these lines. Jesus always addressed the Father in the same vocabulary used in ordinary speech. By all means, we would expect Jesus to have touched upon the proper position of the body that a person should assume when praying! In the mind of some people this is *the* crucial aspect of proper prayer parlance. The following peom fittingly characterizes the prevailing attitude.

> "The proper way for a man to pray,"
>   Said Deacon Lemuel Keyes,
> "And the only proper attitude
>   Is down upon his knees."
>
> "No, I should say the way to pray,"
>   Said Reverend Mr. Wise,

"Is standing straight with outstretched arms,
   And solemn upturned eyes."

"Oh, no, no, no," said Elder Snow,
"Such posture is too proud:
   A man should pray with eyes fast closed
   And head contritely bowed."

"It seems to me his hands should be
   Serenely clasped in front,
   With both thumbs pointing to the ground,"
   Said Reverend Mr. Blunt.

"Last year I fell in Hodgkin's well
   Head first," said Farmer Brown,
"With both my feet a-stickin' up
   And head a-pointin' down:

"And I prayed hard, right then and there—
   Best prayer I ever said.
   The prayin'est prayer I ever prayed
   Was standin' on my head."

AUTHOR UNKNOWN

From my study of New Testament prayer, I would have to agree with the sentiment of Farmer Brown. The position of the body is at best secondary.

Christ began His prayer instruction with the words, "When ye pray, say . . ." (v. 2). So, at the very outset, it becomes evident that prayer is a precise *act* rather than a nebulous communal *attitude* as so often prayers are construed to be today. There is nothing wrong with having a communal attitude with God, but we must never confuse the attitude with the act. Prayer as practiced in the New Testament always had times of definite beginning and ending. It is an act, not performed in cold ritualism, but in intimate

converse with the heavenly Father. The word *Father,* as uttered
by Christ, is fraught with filial intimacy. The most startling aspect
of New Testament prayer practice is that of direct intimate filial
address to one's own loving Father. This is the way Christ prayed
and the way He taught us to pray. We are not to address an
awesome Deity way "out there" but we are called upon to address a deeply concerned Father who is vitally interested in every
aspect of our life and desires supremely to give us "good things"
(Matthew 7:11).

Next, it is self-evident that prayer is essentially petition. It is not
basically praise, adoration, or thanksgiving (although these things
legitimately can be included in prayer). It is asking the Father for
things! We say this because the model prayer Christ gave His
disciples (the Lord's Prayer), is 100 percent petition!

After the brief word of address to the Father, Christ launched
into six model petitions. In fact the whole lesson is on how to
effectively ask God for things. In verses 2-4 of Luke, He teaches
them the types of things for which they should petition the Father.
In verses 5-8 He reveals the proper attitude of the petitioner. We
should ask with the fervency of one beating on his neighbor's
door. In verses 9-13 He lets us know what will happen if we ask
the Father in this way. So, in response to a request, "Lord, teach
us to pray," Jesus taught them *what* to ask for, *how* to ask for it,
and *what* would happen if they asked in this manner! Prayer is
essentially petition. The pious-sounding notion that petitionary
praying is selfish is revealed as a complete fraud when studied in
the light of the New Testament. When Christ prayed, He peti-
tioned almost without exception. When He taught prayer, His
lessons always assumed a petitionary motif. Christ never taught
thanksgiving, praise, or adoration, but He did teach us how to ask!

His six model petitions fall into two obvious groups. The first
three petitions center around the outworking of God's program.
Thus it is self-evident that much of our prayer effort should center
in this area. This would include such things as petitions on behalf

of our local church, our pastor, missionaries, evangelistic endeavors, et cetera. The most amazing thing about these first three petitions is that they all are petitions for things that are providential certainties! God's name will be hallowed! God's Kingdom will most certainly come, and ultimately God's will most certainly will be done not only in heaven but also on earth! Why then pray for such matters? Yet a study of the prayers of both Paul and Christ will reveal that such was unquestionably their practice. Why we should do it I know not, but certainly we are instructed to pray for such matters.

The final three petitions center around the believers' own personal needs. A study of the teachings of the Lord will reveal that no personal need is too great or too insignificant to escape the sphere of legitimate petition. We are addressing a heavenly Father whose concern for us reaches even to the numeric quantity of our head hairs! Dare we think anything too trivial? We are addressing a God who upholds the universe! Dare we assume anything to be beyond His power?

Yet, having said this, it becomes evident both from the model prayer and from the practices of the New Testament that prayers were voiced for significant issues. To pray for obvious trivialities is in a sense like approaching the president of the United States with an assurance from him that any legitimate request would be granted and then asking him for postage stamps!

It also becomes abundantly clear that biblical praying should *essentially* be for spiritual issues. This is not because prayer for material needs is wrong. That they are not is evidenced by the fourth petition, "Give us this day our daily bread." But man's real problems are in the realm of the spiritual. Thus, five out of the six petitions are for spiritual realities. Virtually all of Christ's praying centered in the spiritual. Paul, when praying for believers, always prayed for their spiritual needs. By way of example, the apostle, in praying for the saints at Colossae, voiced seven petitions (*see* Colossians 1:9-12), and all were for their spiritual needs. No doubt there were financial problems in that church; no doubt there were physical needs in that church; no doubt there were people who needed jobs in that church, but you never find Paul praying for this type of thing. Paul saw their real needs as spiritual! How different all of this is from current prayer practice. Listen to the prayer requests next time in an average prayer meeting and you will discover that from 75 to 95 percent are for material needs. When we pray for our church, it is for the mortgage payment; when we pray for our missionaries, it is for a new truck needed on the field; when we pray for our brothers and sisters, it is that they may be delivered from gallstones, varicose veins, or some other physical ailment. Do not misunderstand me. It is not wrong to pray for mortgages, trucks, gallstones, or varicose veins, but such praying reflects an almost complete obliviousness to the real problems. Your church has more serious problems than mortgages. Your missionaries have far greater needs than trucks. Your brother has greater needs than removal of gallstones! We are engaged in a titanic spiritual struggle with "principalities and powers" under subtle satanic direction. We need to ask the Father to open our eyes! We need to be made aware of our real problems! We need spiritual knowledge and discernment. We need spiritual strength. We need to grow in love. Perhaps we need to ask for our eyes to be opened so that we can be increasingly aware of our real problems. Certainly the basic motive for prayer is a sense of dependence and an awareness of need! Thus it logically follows that until and unless we see the real needs, we will not pray meaningfully for those needs.

After instructing the disciples with regard to the types of issues for which they were to petition the Father, Christ immediately gave the parable of the importunate friend (Luke 11:5-8). In this parable the Lord teaches us the *manner* in which petitions are to be voiced. He advocates that petitionary prayer be voiced with the driving urgency of a man beating on a friend's door at midnight in almost shameless effrontery! The man in the parable was in trouble. Crisis pervades the entire scene! This is the mood in which effective petitions are to be voiced to the Father. Crisis pervades almost every prayer setting in the earthly life and teachings of Jesus. So intense was the crisis, so desperate the situation, that the objections from the neighbor within did not stop the persistent cry for assistance. A man in real trouble will not only be bold, desperate, and urgent in his petitions, but he will persist. This is precisely how Christ always taught us to voice petitions to the Father! In another parable (*see* Luke 18:1-8), the Lord pictured prayer under the analogy of a desperate widow pleading before an unjust judge. Though rebuffed repeatedly in her petition, she kept hounding the judge until overwhelmed by the sheer weight of her persistence, the judge was persuaded to grant her request. Under such an analogy Christ taught that persistency in petition was necessary in effective prayer.

Persistent asking, however, must never be confused with vain repetition. Christ taught the former but condemned the latter. His criticism was never against repeating petitions as such, but against vain repetitions. Indeed, Christ Himself repeated the same petition in almost identical language three times in the Garden of Gethsemane. Vain repetitions involve the false notion that God will be heard by much speaking—that the very act of repeating a request is itself meritorious. On the other hand, importunate petition is vastly different in that it is prompted by the very burden of the heart. It is driven by the force of an almost overpowering sense of urgency which must continue to cry out repeatedly day after day. Thus it was with the widow before the judge; thus it was with the man petitioning his neighbor at midnight.

Hence, Christ set forth prayer in graphic terms of driving, earnest, sincere, desperate petition. This is hardly the picture that comes to mind in the familiar hymn "Sweet Hour of Prayer." It becomes evident that we are not really praying simply by mouthing noble petitions on behalf of missionaries. To run through a prayer list with its various petitions each morning as a matter of routine is useless, if not an effrontery to God. It borders on vain repetitions. It is valueless to pray for the pygmies in Africa when we are not really burdened for those pygmies. You are not really praying until you can voice petitions with a sincere sense of urgent need and deep concern.

Friend, if you are living in this tragic world that is fast falling apart, and you are not really concerned about anything, then you ought to be concerned about your own tragic apathy! Until you are concerned, you are only deceiving yourself; you are not engaging in New Testament prayer. I am persuaded that many, if not most, Christians would be far better off to tear up their sweet pious prayer lists, take a fresh piece of paper and write four words on it: "Lord, burden my heart!" Maybe, in addition, they might write: "Lord, open my eyes to significant needs!" Then let that believer keep crying out to God for a burdened heart until he is truly concerned about significant issues. The New Testament knows nothing of simply mouthing insincere, unconcerned petitions. Real prayer is from a vortex of crisis which evokes specific, sincere, and earnest petitions. Prayer prompted by such a burdened heart will persist, will keep asking, will keep knocking day after day.

To that one who does urgently persist, the Lord gives the promise: "For every one that asketh receiveth; and he that seeketh findeth; and to him that knocketh it shall be opened" (Luke 11:10). Thus it is apparent that God will always answer this kind of praying with infallible certainty. In His own way in His own time, the Father always answers authentic New Testament praying. If you doubt the veracity of prayer, you can, by the same logic, doubt your salvation, because they are both based upon the same thing—the *sure promises of God.*

To strengthen further this promise, the Lord uses the analogy of human fathers. Just as an earthly father can be trusted not to deceive his small children by giving stones for bread or serpents for fish (Luke 11:11, 12), so much more we can trust our heavenly

not hesitate to ask because we are in Christ and can petition in His name. This means also that we petition by His authority and with His power. Think of that! I can now petition the Father with all the authority of Christ! What a privilege! What an opportunity! It's like placing a draft on the bank of heaven with the check actually signed by Jesus Christ! That is what it means to pray in His name. I don't ask in my name and on the basis of who I am. Rather, I ask in His name and on the basis of who He is.

Are you beginning to see the astounding possibilities of prayer? Can you see why Christ spent so much time teaching His disciples the fine art of prayer? Can you now see why Christ said that our primary responsibility in this age is to ask? It is because prayer is the divinely ordained means whereby God moves in the accomplishment of His mighty operations on this planet. "If ye ask . . . I will do!" This is the formula that worked in the first-century church, and it has never failed to function, either individually or corporately, for two thousand years whenever God's people have dared to apply it! Every great revival has had its origin in prayer. The Bible records that the weather was changed because a man prayed, wombs were opened because women prayed, battles were won because people prayed, and people were released from prison because of prayer. I am happy to report that God is still in the prayer answering business. I have fantastic documentations for this in my files. I have personally proven the veracity of prayer. I will not give any personal illustrations because it might prove embarrassing to some of the principals. Perhaps one modern example that does not involve me personally will suffice.

A few years ago a young accountant was walking to work and passed the local high school. He heard and saw things that broke his heart. He began praying for that campus. Daily he would pray as he walked past the front of the school. After some weeks he felt so burdened that he formed the habit of walking all the way around the campus before proceeding to work—praying earnestly all the while. After some time he just felt constrained to invite into his home those young people from the campus that he knew. Now this chap was slight of build and introverted and had none of the qualities we usually attribute to a successful youth worker. The few young people he knew on that campus were such social misfits that he later called them "basket cases." At any rate, he gathered these few teen-agers into his home and they simply read the Bible and prayed. He did not know anything else to do. They determined to meet again the following week. Amazingly the thing caught on. In subsequent weeks they filled his home. They had to move the meetings to larger quarters. Leaders on the campus were converted and revival swept the school. One day the bookkeeper received a phone call from one of the members of the city council who said, "I don't know what you have done to my son but I want to take you out to lunch and talk with you." He had the thrill of introducing the city councilman to the Lord.

Yes, Christian, God is still in the prayer answering business. Quietly, irresistibly, unassumingly God answers prayer. Often it is answered in such seemingly natural fashion that you do not realize that an actual prayer miracle is taking place.

Paul said, "Be instant in prayer." James said, "You have not because you ask not." Jesus said, "If you ask . . . I will do." Now people, it either works or it doesn't. The Bible is either telling the truth or it isn't. I challenge you to put God's Word to a simple test and find out for yourself. When a problem arises, when something needs to be done, pray! Instead of doing, ask! Instead of organizing a committee, agonize! I am persuaded that if we had more agonizing and less organizing among the saints, more would be accomplished for God's glory. I know that the human thing to do as situations arise is *act,* but God says *ask,* and He will act. I know it doesn't make sense humanly speaking, but God has a way of making good sense out of nonsense. Try it! I'm positive that you will be amazed and pleased. *Prayer is where the action is!*

9

Separation or Isolation

A vital part of practical Christian living is reaching out to the unsaved. We all have neighbors, business associates, or fellow students with whom we are in contact daily. What should our attitude be toward those who have yet to know the joy of salvation?

In this chapter we will take a serious look at a concept long hallowed by evangelical Christians. Let's consider the matter of "separation from the world." If I asked you, "Are you a separated Christian?" You would probably say yes. But what does it mean to be a separated Christian? More particularly, what does the Bible teach us about separation? I find that when most Christians say they are separated from the world they mean they are isolated from the "nasty" world of the unsaved. For many, the idea of separation is a pious escape from reality, an excuse for not being aggressively involved in the very world we are called upon to reach for Christ.

Does the Bible teach any kind of separation? Is it legitimate to even study this subject? 1 John 2:15 states, "Love not the world, neither the things that are in the world. If any man love the world, the love of the Father is not in him." Here is something called the *world* and we are not supposed to love it. Also in this connection notice 2 Corinthians 6:17, ". . . come out from among them, and be ye separate, saith the Lord, and touch not the unclean thing."

Again in James 4:4, "Ye adulterers and adulteresses, know ye not
that the friendship of the world is enmity with God? whosoever
therefore will be a friend of the world is the enemy of God." The
language is explicit and clear. If language means anything, there
is something dangerous about the world, its ways, its thinking, and
its values! The Christian who gets too friendly with the world
becomes miserable and useless, so there is a legitimate biblical
sense in which we should be separated from the world.

As we indicated earlier, when most Christians say they are
"separated Christians" they mean an almost total isolation from
the world. Traditional isolationism operates on two propositions.
In saying he is separated from the world, the isolationist means
first of all he is *separated from sin.* However, he carries his logic
a step further and not only separates himself from sin, but *separates himself from the sinner!* In other words, he will have as little
contact with sinful men as possible, and all under the pious sound-
ing phrase, "I am a separated Christian. I am separated from the
world." The isolationist will develop his own exclusive society of
the saved. He will seek to make his little world as airtight as
possible and have minimal contact with unsaved people! What do
we tell our new converts? We tell them to drop all of their unsaved
friends, fearing that the new believer will be contaminated by old
influences.

Now isolationism is not new. Way back in the Middle Ages
certain people decided they wanted to be separated from the
world. They went out into the boondocks, built high walls, and
totally isolated themselves from the world. Today it is called
monasticism. I submit to you that today the evangelical church is
largely monastic. We don't have walls of brick or stone, but we
do have our walls. We have become sort of a monastic mutual
admiration society where we sit around singing and patting each
other on the back while the rest of the world is going to perdition.
I know of one community where the saints developed a Christian
Businessmen's directory. If a believer in that town has motor

trouble, he doesn't need to contaminate himself with a nasty old unsaved mechanic. All he need do is consult his directory and he can have a nice clean Christian work on his car. I have seen advertisements for Christian retirement homes where saints were assured of breathing the clean, clear air of Christian fellowship seven days a week! All of this is pure monastic philosophy. Is this what the Bible means by being separated from the world? I am persuaded it is not!

The classic error in such thinking is its opposition to the great commission. How is one going to carry out the great commission and be a consistent isolationist? How are we to make disciples of all people? How are we to preach the gospel to every creature if we have as little contact with them as we possibly can? Our philosophy of separation is at cross-purposes with our philosophy of missions. All year long out of one side of our mouths we say that we are separated Christians. We don't invite our neighbors over for dinner because they might contaminate us. We don't go hunting and fishing with our neighbors. We have as little contact as we can with these neighbors. Then one week an evangelist comes to our town. It is *our* week of evangelism. So over to the neighbors we go and knock on the door with an invitation to the evangelistic meetings. We have a fat chance of success when we haven't really made an effort to associate with him in a meaningful way all year long. Do we realize that on one hand we are saying, be separated from the world, yet on the other hand we are saying, win the world for Jesus? Our view of separation is at cross-purposes with our teaching on evangelism!

As a Bible teacher I am asked to speak for special church meetings and conferences. In a church where I had been asked to speak, I was billed as an evangelist instead of a Bible teacher. They had extensively advertised the week of meetings to be held in their church. At the opening meeting on Sunday morning, the pastor urged the people to support the week of evangelistic effort. He said, ''Now folks, I want all of you to go out this week and invite all of your unsaved friends." Well, they didn't have any unsaved friends! He had taught them for ten years not to have any unsaved friends. Yet during the week of evangelism they were challenged to invite out all of their unsaved friends. This points out a great evangelical inconsistency.

Study the life of Christ. When He wasn't teaching His disciples, He was associating with unsaved people. He was accused of being a friend of publicans and sinners. In John 4 we read that He deliberately went through Samaria to make contact with an un-saved woman. The woman was the kind that most men would not want to be seen with in broad daylight. She had gone through five husbands, and the man she was living with was not her husband. Yet, Jesus deliberately made contact with her for the purpose of reaching her. Christ was not an isolationist.

Isolationism leads to a pale, pallid Christianity. I think the aver-age Christian today is quite bored with his monastic Christian life. He mechanically goes through his little routine of going to church, Sunday school, and prayer meeting. He must look to the occa-sional Sunday-school contest to relieve his boredom.

Can you imagine the Apostle Paul being bored? When he went into a town he checked out the local jail because he knew that's where he would probably end up. Paul knew every jailer by his first name. He was beaten half to death and shipwrecked. He lived dangerously for Christ, but it surely wasn't boring! It was gripping and thrilling and exciting! Paul was not a monastic. He wasn't practicing isolationism. When Paul came into town he went to the city square where he could meet unsaved people and make contact with them.

There is yet another view concerning the Christian's relation-ship to the world that is currently coming to prominence. It is really a reaction to traditional isolationism. This reaction is particu-larly prevalent among younger people. However, when young people react, they often overreact. I call this overreaction to tradi-tional isolationism *integration*. The integrationist has two propositions. He says, "Associate with sinners. Someone has to reach the unsaved. You stuffy older people just keep Jesus Christ bottled up in your churches and never associate with sinners." However, while he advocates associating with sinners, he carries his logic a step further. He not only associates with sinners, but also associates with their *sin*. In other words, a complete integration with this world and its ways, a complete identification with the sinner. Such young people have advocated such things as "beer and Bible study." They tell us that one must get right down with the unsaved and live on their level in order to really reach them.

A young man came to me one day complaining about the hypocrites in his church who were too self-righteous to be bothered with the sinners in the community. He said, "Somebody has to reach the sinners down in Joe's Bar." He then declared himself a missionary to Joe's Bar. He went down there and began to freely associate with the sinners. He not only associated with them, but he also freely associated with their sin. The last time I saw the young man, it looked like the fellows at Joe's Bar had done a pretty good missionary job on him! He was rather well juiced up (drunk).

Let's evaluate integrationism. There is so much that is obviously wrong with the integrationists' view that I almost feel like the proverbial mosquito in the nudist colony. I don't know where to strike first. Probably the best thing we could say by way of biblical refutation would be the words of Titus 2:14, where Christians are referred to as "peculiar people." The expression *peculiar* does not mean "odd ball." It means a unique person, a distinct person. If we are going to have an impact upon this world, we must be unique. If we participate in all of their sin and act just like they do, we are not going to have any impact on them whatsoever. If we wallow in the same pigpen morality with the unsaved, we will never influence them for Christ!

Perhaps you are thinking about now, "Well, what *is* the answer?" Isolationism fails to reach the unsaved in a meaningful way. Integrationism falls into the sinful ways of the unsaved. Neither one is effective. The biblical position is to be found by finding the truth in both positions. The biblical view is not isolation or integration, but *infiltration!* We must admit that the young people are right when they advocate association with sinners. In fact I would make it even stronger. I would say we should *deliberately* associate with sinners. I use the term deliberately because you will find that the old adage, "Birds of a feather flock together" is true. You will not naturally gravitate toward unsaved people, and they will not naturally gravitate toward you. We tend to gravitate toward people who have the same world view that we have. We tend to gravitate toward people who have the same set of values we have. You will find unsaved people are very leery of you. We must deliberately take the initiative to create friendships with unsaved people for the purpose of winning them. Did Jesus teach this? I believe He did. In Matthew 5:13-15, He said, "Ye are the salt of the earth: but if the salt have lost his savour, wherewith shall it be salted? it is thenceforth good for nothing, but to be cast out, and to be trodden under foot of men. Ye are the light of the world. A city that is set on an hill cannot be hid. Neither do men light a candle, and put it under a bushel. . . ." Oh, don't they? That is exactly what the isolationist has been doing for years. Boy, do we ever let our light shine in prayer meeting. But we are to let our light shine *before men.*

Jesus said that His disciples were to function as *salt* and *light.* Salt and light have one common characteristic—penetration! It is the function of the salt to penetrate the meat with something it desperately needs, and it is the function of light to penetrate the darkness with something it desperately needs. Jesus is saying that as His disciples, we are to penetrate the world. We are not to bottle up our Christianity inside the four walls of our church. Rather we are to penetrate this world with something it desperately needs.

Jesus said if we fail to penetrate we are "good for nothing, but . . . to be trodden under foot of men." I submit to you we have failed to penetrate and as a result, the world is indeed walking all over us! They have no real respect for us. The world has more respect for the radicals like the Black Panthers, Weathermen, or SDS than they do for the average Christian. It is not because the world agrees with the radical. But in the radical they see a person who is not afraid to be inconvenienced for his convictions. They see a man who is not afraid to go to jail for what he believes, and they respect that. How is the Christian viewed? I'm afraid the world views us as a bunch of nice people sitting around doing nothing in particular. If anybody ought to be radical, in the wholesome sense, it ought to be the church of Jesus Christ. However, all too often we sit Sunday after Sunday just watching the show!

Ask God to show you creative ways to make meaningful contact with the people with whom you work. Instead of going to a football game with another Christian friend, invite the guy who works next to you in the shop to go along. You won't have nearly as good a time. In fact, you might just be miserable. He'll possibly smoke up your car with his cigarettes and you will be on edge all evening because you're not sure when he will say something off-color, and you won't know just how to respond. Yes, you would have a much more enjoyable evening with a Christian, but we are not on this earth to have a good time. We are on this earth to do a job for God.

Did you ever think of volunteering to serve in a voter registration booth just to have an opportunity to make contact with people? Why not attend PTA meetings for the same reason. If you are a student, enter into wholesome school activities for the same reason. You will make contact with people who would never attend your church. Deliberately associate with them for the purpose of reaching them.

Now all of this will not be easy. Some of their habits will irritate you. You won't like some of their ways of thinking. You may be uncomfortable. This last year my wife and I invited an unsaved couple with whom we had become acquainted to go to the county fair with us. Frankly, I had a miserable evening. I would have had a much more enjoyable evening with another Christian couple, but we're not on this earth just to have a good time. Love is willing to make sacrifices and to give of itself for the sake of the person loved. With the love of Christ constraining us, we've been commissioned to go out into the highways and byways and compel them to come in.

We must deliberately associate with the unsaved, but we must be very careful not to be completely like them. Traditional Christianity is right when it insists we must separate ourselves from sin. There *must* be a separation from sin. The real idea in biblical separation is not disassociation, but distinction. We must go out and associate with the men of this world, but remain *distinct.* We must have the intestinal fortitude to be different! Christ did this. He associated with sinners, yet He could stand at the end of a three-year public ministry and say, "Which of you convinceth me of sin?" (John 8:46). He was distinct from their sin. This is biblical separation—deliberately associating with them, but remaining separate from their sin.

A great example of real separation is Daniel. As a teen-ager he was hauled off to a bad culture. The Babylonians were polluted pagans. They had their booze and broads; their topless this and bottomless that. What did Daniel do? Did he get together with all of his Jewish friends and say, "Look fellows. We must live here among these nasty old Babylonians, but let's have as little contact with them as we possibly can. Let's form a little holy club." Is that what he did? No! You read the record. He took on a Babylonian name. He dressed like the Babylonians. He even got into Babylonian politics and was very successful. However, did Daniel ever compromise with their sin? Never! They told him that if anyone prayed to anyone else other than the king for thirty days, he would be made into lion food. Yet in the face of this threat Daniel proceeded with boldness to pray! That's biblical separation. Dare to be a Daniel. Dare to stand alone. Dare to have a purpose firm. Dare to make it known. This is infiltration—actually getting out and having the courage to be different.

Now, let's get right down to cases. I want to challenge you to associate with your neighbors and people you work with. When you are on the job and it's lunch time, invite an unsaved person to join you for lunch. But when you sit down to eat, I hope you'll bow your head and thank God for the food. I hope you won't start gobbling it down like all the other animals around you. Yet don't stand up like some pious Pharisees and say, "Let us pray." Ask God to help you be sharp in the process of being different. On the other hand, don't just cop out and act like you've suddenly contracted a migraine headache and start massaging your temples while faking a prayer. Or don't allow your napkin to slip off your lap and then reach down to get it and pray on the way up! Simply bow your head and thank God for your food. Your luncheon companion will probably say, "What's wrong, are you sick?" Look him squarely in the eye and say, "No, I believe that God provided this food. I believe that God provided a body that can assimilate this food and believe it only makes sense to thank Him, don't you?" You will have thereby borne testimony to the fact that you are unique and that you are not like all of the pagans around you that just inhale their food with no regard for God.

Another example: when someone visits you on a Sunday afternoon and it comes time for church, what should you do? I'll tell you what to do. You tell them enthusiastically that you have a fantastic church service on Sunday evening and would like to have them come along. They will do one of two things. Either they will go with you, or they will go home. Either way you have registered that God is important to you.

Dare to be different. Ask God to help you think of opportunities to make contact with unsaved people. I know of one minister who was a carpenter before he became a Christian. He hasn't professionally driven a nail in twenty years, but he is still a member of the Carpenters' Union and goes to union meetings. Why? To make contact with unsaved men! Until a short time ago I maintained a license to sell insurance in the state of California. I haven't sold insurance in years, but I kept up the fee so I could contact the unsaved. I have discovered over the years that there is a professional stigma about preachers. When I sit down next to a fellow in a restaurant and start talking to him, invariably he would ask the question, "What do you do for a living?" If I said, "I am a preacher," immediately he would clam up and I couldn't talk to him anymore because I was out of his league. However, if I could say that I had a license to sell insurance in the state of California then I was still in the ball game.

I want to warn you not to participate in authentic biblical separation unless you are in the peak spiritually. This is no job for cowards. This is no job for spiritual weaklings. It's going to take courage. It's going to take spiritual strength. I mean this is really getting out where the action is! You need to be prayed up. You must be living in a close relationship with your Lord. It's exciting, but it's dangerous.

If you begin to practice infiltration, I can tell you what to expect. You can expect persecution! But is persecution so unusual? Didn't they persecute Christ? Was Paul persecuted? Were the apostles persecuted? All of them met a violent death except the Apostle John, and he was shipped off to an island in the Mediterranean Sea. Notice the words of 2 Timothy 3:12, "Yea, and all that will live godly in Christ Jesus shall suffer persecution." Have you been persecuted lately? Why not? If you are not being persecuted, then something is wrong. They persecuted Christ. They are going to persecute you. I am not saying we should have a persecution complex, but if we live godly lives in the midst of a godless society, then persecution in one form or another will come. It may not always be physical. In our culture many times it is emotional or psychological, but it will be there if we are living the way we should live and doing what we should do! If you are operating month after month and nobody is hitting you with a tomato or persecuting you in some manner, something is wrong. If you are an isolationist and not making meaningful contact with the unsaved, then certainly no one will persecute you. Nobody is persecuted in a monastery. On the other hand, if you are associating with unsaved people but compromising with their sin, you will not be persecuted either. If we are really associating with the unsaved and daring to be different, then persecution will occur and should be expected.

Perhaps someone is saying, "Isn't that dangerous?" Sure it's dangerous. Christians are taught to "Put on the whole armour of God" (Ephesians 6:11). Why do we put on armor? Is it to go to a Sunday-school picnic? You put on armor to go into battle! Most Christians, however, put on the whole armor of God and then go to prayer meeting. It reminds me of a statement I once heard attributed to Peter Marshall. It went something like this: "Today's Christians are like deep-sea divers encased in suits designed for many fathoms deep; marching bravely forth to pull plugs out of bathtubs." We sing, "Onward Christian soldiers, marching as to war," and go to the evening church service. The average group of Christians reminds me of a football team in a perpetual huddle. We meet together and discuss strategy, but nobody ever gets out on the line of scrimmage. That's where the action is! That's where it's dangerous, to be sure, but that's also where it is meaningful, gripping, and exciting!

Another brother might say, "But aren't there problems?" Sure there are problems. In practicing biblical separation you will encounter many problems. Who ever said that the Christian life was easy? If you go out each week seeking, with God's help, to make meaningful contact with unsaved people, you will have all kinds of problems! There will be times when you will fail, but that's wonderful because it will drive you to your knees. They are going to ask questions you won't be able to answer, but that can be good because it can compel you to turn to the Bible to find the answers. You'll have a sense of your own weakness and inadequacy as you've never had before, but that can be beneficial because it will teach you to depend upon the Holy Spirit as never before.

This is biblical separation. This is thrilling, aggressive New Testament Christianity. Men are dying and we can no longer isolate ourselves. The church of Jesus Christ needs a new theme song. For much too long we have been singing, "When the saints go marching in. . . ." It's time the saints started marching out! We've kept Jesus Christ bottled up within the four walls of our church much too long! We must go out and associate with sinners no matter how little they encourage us. We must make ourselves expendable for Christ's cause. We must learn to talk with them about fashions and sports and politics until we get a chance to speak of something far more wonderful—Jesus Christ.

I don't mean that you need feel compelled to present the gospel on the first encounter with an unsaved person. Be patient, gain their confidence and friendship, wait prayerfully for the right opportunity. In fact, you may find on the first encounter that they are expecting you to unload on them. For that reason they may demonstrate a marked uneasiness. If you invite your unsaved neighbors over for dinner, that first evening they may act like people sitting on a time bomb. If you sense this, by all means do not even speak of spiritual things that evening. Let them know you are human, but don't compromise with their sin. They will actually be disappointed in you if you compromise. You may interact with them socially for months, building a relationship, before the right opportunity arrives.

Constantly remind yourself of your goal. You are not socializing as an end in itself, but as a means to a more significant end. You have something they need desperately. They may not even realize they need it. You are gaining their friendship and confidence because you are really interested in them as individuals and want to see them receive the most wonderful gift of all—". . . eternal life through Jesus Christ our Lord" (Romans 6:23).

To be sure this type of aggressive biblical separation will cause you inconvenience and sacrifice, but the rewards are manifold. Your Christian life will take on new excitement. As you go forth each day prayerfully seeking to make contacts with unsaved people, you will never know exactly what to expect. You will find you must constantly stay in close dependence upon the Lord to survive. I have never known a person to practice this kind of aggressive biblical separation and be bored with his Christian life. Life isn't a drab, colorless routine when you are in daily contact with the enemy (perhaps it would be better to say, "beloved enemy"). This is thrilling, aggressive New Testament Christianity. This is the sower *going forth to sow* (*see* Matthew 13).

Our world is falling apart. We have been commissioned to go into the highways and hedges and bid them to come (*see* Luke 14:23). We dare not remain in our monasteries a moment longer.

10

Let's All Wear the Badge

While talking with a group of Christians some time ago, a young woman mentioned, with great elation, that after working in a particular company for a number of months, just the day before she had discovered that there was another believer working in the same company. She then made the following observation: "Wouldn't it be wonderful if we Christians had a badge by which we could be identified." I pointed out that we do have a badge, and turned to the following passage of Scripture, "A new commandment I give unto you, That ye love one another; as I have loved you, that ye also love one another. By this shall all men know that ye are my disciples, if ye have love one to another" (John 13:34,35).

This statement is most interesting. It is part of what we call the Upper Room discourse. Jesus and His disciples were in the Upper Room. Judas the traitor had gone. Christ had washed the disciples' feet and had instituted the Lord's Supper. In this obviously intimate setting, He began to talk to them. In the verses immediately preceding the new commandment, He talked about His departure via the cross and Ascension (v. 31-34). Then, following Peter's interruption (verses 36-38), the Lord speaks of returning again in what we now know to be the Rapture (14:1-3). Do you now see the setting of the new commandment? Just before He gives the new commandment, He speaks of going away. Then immediately after giving the new commandment, He speaks of coming again. Between the fact that He is going away and that He is going to come back again, Christ presents this new commandment.

It seems as if the new commandment is to be the governing principle that should guide Christians between the time that He goes away and the time He comes back. It's somewhat like a football coach. He's been training his men for months and now it is time for the first football game. According to the rules of the sport, the coach must be separated from the players. He cannot go out on the field with his men until half time. So he gathers his athletes together and gives some final words of instruction. He tells them the things he wants them to keep in mind until he is able to meet with them again at half time. My high-school football coach had so many things he wanted to tell us in those moments that he wrote out notes on paper to remind himself of all of the things that he wanted to tell us. But our Lord had just *one* thing to tell His followers. He had trained them. He was going to leave them and He wanted them to keep but one thing in mind until He came back again for them. "A new commandment I give unto you, That ye love one another; as I have loved you, that ye also love one another. By this shall all men know that ye are my disciples, if ye have love one to another."

Christ gave them a new *commandment.* A commandment is a precept, principle, or instruction to govern a person's life. Some have called this the eleventh commandment; but Christ did not call it another commandment, He called it a *new* commandment. It is a new commandment to a new group of people. We have here a unique commandment for His "little children" (13:33).

The content of this commandment is *love.* Love is a major theme in the Bible. The one verse that characterizes the message of the Bible more completely than any other single statement is John 3:16, "For God so loved the world, that he gave his only begotten Son, that whosoever believeth in him should not perish, but have everlasting life."

It is important for us to understand exactly what the Bible means when it tells us to love one another. In our culture, we often have only a romantic concept of love. You know, boy meets girl, heart palpitation, moon in June, and so forth. Notice, however, that Christ says we are to love one another, as He loved us. I hate to disillusion any of you, but when the Bible says that God loves you, it doesn't mean that God's heart skips a beat every time He looks at you. The word for "love" most often used in the New Testament depicting divine love carries the concept of *practical concern* rather than romantic infatuation. By way of example, the same word is used in Ephesians 5, with reference to husbands loving their wives. Now it is true that husbands are to love their wives in a romantic way, but that is obviously not the main thrust that is being taught in that chapter. Notice Paul's statement, "Husbands, love your wives as your own body . . ." (*see* Ephesians 5:28). The husband is to love his wife as he loves his body. How do we love our bodies? We don't have a romantic infatuation for our bodies. We don't stand in front of a mirror and drool over our beautiful bodies! At least I hope no one does. If you do, you're in trouble! If you get your kicks out of flexing your muscles and admiring yourself, you really need help. No, you do not have a romantic infatuation for your body. You have a practical concern for your body. When you stub your toe, you don't smother it with kisses, you put a bandage on it. That's the way men are to love their wives. Some men love their wives romantically, but not in this practical way.

So when the Bible says that God loves you, it means that He has a practical concern for your welfare. The command for us to love one another means that we are to have a practical concern for each other. One of the best illustrations of what John really means when he says we are to love one another is found in his first Epistle, "But whoso hath this world's good, and seeth his brother have need, and shutteth up his bowels of compassion from him, how dwelleth the love of God in him? My little children,

let us not love in word, neither in tongue; but in deed and in truth"
(1 John 3:17, 18). What's he saying? He is simply saying that if you
have money in the bank and food in your cupboard and it comes
to your attention that a Christian brother has real material needs
and all you do is say with your mouth that you love him, but do
not do anything in a tangible way to help that brother, how can
you have the audacity to say that you love him? Real love ex-
presses itself in deeds. Paul was essentially referring to the same
thing when he said, ". . . be ye kind one to another, tenderhearted,
forgiving one another, even as God for Christ's sake hath forgiven
you" (Ephesians 4:32). A good synonym for the biblical idea of
love would be *caring*. To love one another is to really care about
one another and the proof of real caring love is demonstrated in
sacrificial giving. If we really care we will give of ourselves and
our substance for our brothers. This is what the new commandment really means.

Now why did our Lord evidently feel that it was so crucial for
His disciples to love one another? He goes on to tell us in the very
next verse, "By this shall all men know that ye are my disciples,
if ye have love one to another" (John 13:35). The reason He wants
us to love one another is that this is the way men will really know
that we are His disciples. Love is a badge. Love is the identifying
mark of a genuine disciple of Jesus. Love is the credential of a
Christian.

Let's suppose that next Sunday all of us are gathered together
in a public worship service when suddenly the door bursts open
and a man charges down the middle aisle, demanding that we
break up the meeting! We would probably all be so shocked at
first that we wouldn't know what to do. If we had our wits about
us, the very first thing we should do is demand to see his credentials. We would want to see his badge of authority! If he couldn't
produce the badge, then we would probably usher him out of the
meeting. If the man couldn't produce credentials we wouldn't
heed his message. The world has a right to see our badge. "By this

shall all men know that ye are my disciples, if ye have love one to another.''

There are a lot of people in our world claiming to be the bona fide disciples of Jesus Christ. We find the great Eastern Orthodox tradition and they are saying, ''Hear us. We are His disciples!'' Why? ''Well, because we can trace our lineage right back to Palestine. Our church began geographically where Christ lived and died.'' Then there is the Roman Catholic tradition and they say, ''Hear us. We are His disciples!'' Why? ''Because of our apostolic succession. We can trace our popes right back to Peter.'' Finally, there are various Protestant groups. They say, ''No, you hear us! We are His disciples.'' Why? ''Look at our creed. Look at our doctrine.'' I am afraid that in many cases the world stands back in unbelief. The world still awaits unconvinced because they do not see the *badge!*

It is not by geographic location, it is not by apostolic succession, it is not by orthodoxy of doctrine, but it is by a practical demonstration of brotherly love that all men are to know that we are His disciples. You can contend for the faith. You can insist and believe in the verbal inspiration of Scripture, the virgin birth, the Deity of Christ, the Resurrection, even the millenium, but if you do not have love, it's of no avail. It is not enough to be saved or to stand for the fundamentals of the faith, live a separated Christian life, and observe Christian ordinances. We can have all of these, but if we are not wearing the badge, our testimony will be of no avail.

Is this not essentially the message of 1 Corinthians 13? We are told categorically that we can have faith that will remove mountains. We can be so zealous that we can give our bodies to be burned. We can be eloquent preachers. We can have all kinds of knowledge, but if we do not have love, *we are a zero!* If there is no love, all is wasted.

Often we get our witnessing all backwards. Yes, we are to go into all the world and preach the gospel, but in doing so we must be careful to wear the badge. Until and unless they can see our credentials, all of our talk is of little avail. They have a right to demand to see our credentials. So often we are so eager to chalk up another decision for Christ that we really show no real concern for the problems of people. It is possible to busy ourselves passing out tracts, but be insensitive, or even crude individuals.

A friend of mine went into the hospital some time ago. Her doctor, a Christian, came to her as she was about ready to be discharged and told her that he appreciated the way she had conducted herself while in the hospital. She was unaware that she had conducted herself in an unusual manner and asked him what he meant. He explained to her that as a Christian he tried to bear a testimony to members of the staff, but so often his greatest hindrance in witnessing was professed Christian patients. Habitually they came into the hospital with a great big Bible under one arm and a fistful of tracts under the other arm. They placed the Bible and tracts on the nightstand and then proceeded to be the most cantankerous, impossible patients in the hospital. "By this shall all men know that ye are my disciples, if ye have love one to another."

Shortly after my conversion, I was anxious to share my new-found faith with my closest friend. He accepted Christ and was then most anxious to see his father won to the Lord. His father was a life-insurance salesman. After much talk, he persuaded his father to visit the church. At the end of the afternoon I called my friend to see how his father had reacted. He told me that his dad wouldn't go back to that church again. There was a woman at the church who was a client of his father. For years she had been the most difficult, impossible customer that he had ever dealt with. His father concluded that if that was a representation of Christianity he wanted no part of it.

Everyone agrees that the greatest job of evangelism was done by the first-century church. They didn't have much money. They had minimal organizational machinery. How were they so effective in reaching their generation? One reason is that they went forth flashing the badge. They amazed the pagan world by the love that they had for each other. Tradition records such statements as, "My, how these Christians love one another. They seem to love each other before they even know each other." The early church produced the credentials of genuine disciples and the pagans responded.

The sad thing is that so often the very church in the community that is really preaching the Bible is often known as "the fighting fundamentalists." You can count on them to have a good church fight at every business meeting. Periodically they are going to run the preacher out of town. Beloved, these things ought not to be so! Is it any wonder that unsaved people are not convinced?

How have you answered our Lord's command? Have you put on the badge? Are you wearing the badge? Are you really characterized by love for your fellow believer or are you characterized by petty jealousy, pride, self-centeredness, bickering? I am persuaded that if I should close this chapter right now, many of you would put this book down and charge out with the attitude that you are going to love if it kills you, and it probably would. Therefore, I don't want to bring the chapter to a close without discussing *how* we are going to be able to carry out this commandment of our Lord.

You will discover that when the Lord gives a command, a close look at the Word of God will generally give a method by which the command may be carried out. I think one failure of evangelical teaching today lies in the fact that it is so often centered around challenge with little or no discussion of practical implementation. We are challenged to do something and never given any instruction as to how such a challenge may be implemented.

How am I going to obey this commandment? The first thing is to realize that you cannot generate this kind of love by self-effort. This kind of love is a fruit of the Spirit. It is a product of the Holy Spirit that indwells you. For you to think that by self-effort you can generate this kind of love is like expecting apples to suddenly appear on pine trees. You can't do it, and the sooner you realize that the better off you will be. All love of this kind must ultimately come from God. This is brought out in 1 John 4:10: "Herein is love, not that we loved God, but that he loved us. . . ." In other words, the source of love is not our love, but God's love. All love of this kind will find its ultimate source in Him.

But I have good news! While you can never produce this love, Christ prayed that you might have this divine love within you. In John 17:26 we read, ". . . I have declared unto them thy name, and will declare it: that the love wherewith thou hast loved me may be in them, and I in them." Further, I am happy to announce that this prayer has been answered. In Romans 5:5 we read, "And hope maketh not ashamed; because the love of God is shed abroad in our hearts by the Holy Ghost which is given unto us." You have received an injection of love. You have love in you. Perhaps you are saying, "You don't know me very well!" Maybe not, but I know the Scripture and if you are a Christian, you have received an injection of God's love.

However, as long as God's love is bottled up inside of you, it doesn't do your brothers and sisters any good. It must be emitted through your personality. You cannot produce divine love, but divine love can be expressed through your personality. Or, in the words of 1 John 4:12, "If we love one another, God dwelleth in us, and his love is perfected in us." Notice the passive voice of the final verb—"is perfected." It's not something a believer can do, but something that God does through him.

Now how is God able to work out this love through my personality? By submission on my part. I am told to yield myself to the indwelling Holy Spirit. I am told not to quench Him, but to let Him have complete control (see Ephesians 5:18). So the first step in obeying Christ's commandment to love one another is to completely submit to the indwelling Holy Spirit and allow Him to perfect God's love through my personality.

By way of illustration, imagine a pipeline. This pipeline is plugged into a mountain reservoir with a bountiful supply of clear, crystal water. The pipeline runs from the mountain reservoir down into the desert valley. The desert valley desperately needs water. At the end of the pipeline there is a valve. The valve is closed. Now if you could give some advice to the pipeline, what would your instructions be? Would you say, "Pipeline, generate water? Pipeline, produce water?" No. You would say, "Pipeline, open the valve and allow the water to flow through." May I say that that is exactly where you are. You have received an injection of divine love. This love has been given to you. Now you need to let this love come out through your personality. By a definite act of your will, you need to open the valve and submit your total self to the complete control of the Holy Spirit. As this is done, gradually the Holy Spirit will develop through your personality the fruit of the Spirit which is love. Gradually you will begin to care about your brothers and sisters. You will then begin to do something in a tangible way to minister to their needs.

In addition to inward submission, there must be outward active effort on our part. Paul urges us to "follow after charity . . ." (1 Corinthians 14:1). The language is very strong. The believer is to aggressively pursue love. Similarly the writer of the Book of Hebrews admonishes Christians to provoke one another to love (see Hebrews 10:24). The word provoke means to really agitate each other. It is also an extremely strong term. How can we provoke our brothers and sisters to love? There are many practical ways if only we will set our ingenuity to work. One way is to use our actions to change our attitudes. We know that our will has very little control over our emotions. We can't just say that we are going to start feeling kind towards someone that we have felt enmity for. We can't just change our feelings towards that person by our will. So our will has very little control over our emotions, but our will does have a lot of control over our actions. So what we are going to suggest is to provoke one another to love and good works by using our actions which our will can control to change our feelings and attitudes. Let's imagine that two Christian women hate each other. I don't know what women say when they feel that way about each other. Men would say, "They hate each other's guts." Maybe women would say, "They'd like to tear out each other's blond hair by its black roots." In either case, it is a terrible thing to have that kind of animosity among believers. God commands you to love that person and you find it impossible to feel real compassion. What can you do? Here's what you can do. Walk into your kitchen and bake a batch of cookies. That's something you can do. Take the cookies into your car. That's something you can do. Drive over to that Christian's house. That's something you can do. Ring the doorbell and when that lady opens the door, offer her the cookies. I dare say that she will be quite shocked. She will probably invite you in and perhaps over coffee she will begin to share what is on her heart and you will begin to understand why she acts the way she does. She will also get insight into you. You will find your feelings changing towards that woman.

Thus by inward submission, by daily moment-by-moment commitment to the indwelling Holy Spirit, you will gradually be allowing Him to develop love through your personality. Then by positive external action, provoke one another to love and good works. Ask God to help you think of creative ways to stimulate each other to love and good works. Make it a matter of deliberate prayer and you will be amazed at how God will show you innovative ways to pursue love. Then men will begin to notice the bona fide credential of a Christian. They will see your good works and glorify your Father which is in heaven.

The Apostle John, who was the human instrument used to write the passage that we have been studying in this chapter, was the only apostle not to die a violent death. Tradition tells us that he lived to a ripe old age. In his later years John became so feeble that he could no longer walk into the assembly of believers. They would carry him in on a stretcher. On such occasions the Christians would say, "Brother John, preach us a sermon." The old warrior would always respond with the same message that he preached over and over again. It went like this: "My little children, love one another because this is the Lord's commandment, and if only this be fulfilled it is enough."

We've a story to tell to the nations; but if we are going to effectively tell that story, we must display the proper credentials. Let's all wear the badge!